Gender and Human Rights

Gender and Human Rights

Narratives on Macro-Micro Realities

Edited by

Bishnu C. Barik
Pushpesh Kumar
Usha S. Sarode

RAWAT PUBLICATIONS

Jaipur • New Delhi • Bangalore • Guwahati • Kolkata

ISBN 978-81-316-0370-3

Reprinted, 2018

Published by
Prem Rawat for **Rawat Publications**
Satyam Apts, Sector 3, Jawahar Nagar, Jaipur 302 004 (India)
Phone: 0141 265 1748/7006 Fax: 0141 265 1748
E-mail: info@rawatbooks.com
Website: www.rawatbooks.com

New Delhi Office
4858/24, Ansari Road, Daryaganj, New Delhi 110 002
Phone: 011 2326 3290

Also at *Bangalore, Guwahati* and *Kolkata*

Typeset by Rawat Computers, Jaipur

Printed and bound in India.

To

Professor Jaganath Pathy

Former Professor of Sociology, South Gujarat University, Surat

commemorating his contributions to the disciplines of
Sociology and Anthropology

Contents

Acknowledgement

This volume has grown out of two national seminars on “Gender and Human Rights”, organized consecutively by the School of Social Sciences, Swami Ramanand Teerth Marathwada University, Nanded, in the years 2004 and 2005.

We express our sincere thanks and gratitude to the Ministry of Tribal Affairs, Government of India, New Delhi, Ministry of Health and Family Welfare, Government of India, New Delhi, Indian Institute of Human Rights, New Delhi and Swami Ramanand Teerth Marathwada University, Nanded, for providing generous financial support for organizing the above seminars.

We owe a lot to our invited intellectual luminaries, to name them, Dr Asghar Ali Engineer, Dr Rama Melkote, Prof Kalpana Kannabiran, Prof Laxmi Lingam, Prof S.N Chaudhary, Prof Indira Munshi, Prof G. Satyanarayanan, Prof V.N. Bhatt, Ms Vishakha Dutt, Mr Alok Gupta, Dr Wandana Sonalkar and Ms Meera Sadgopal for their enlighten interventions in the proceedings of seminars. We also express our sincere thanks to our delegate friends who presented their papers. This present volume contains only eleven papers selectively chosen out of forty papers presented in the two seminars. We also intend to put on record our sincere thanks and gratitude to our Hon’ble Vice-Chancellor, Prof S.A. Suryawanshi for giving us timely guidance and providing all logistics as and when required.

It is a fact but not exaggeration that the above seminars could not have been decently organized without the enthusiasm shown in and hard work put in by the colleagues in the School, Dr P.M Katare, Dr E.N. Ashok Kumar, Dr A.I Shaikh and Dr G.S. Yelne and of course our students. We express our sincere thanks to all of them.

We owe a special debt to Dr J.M. Waghmare, the founder Vice-Chancellor of this University and presently the Member of Parliament (Rajya Sabha) for his constant advice for conducting such academic activities in the School.

In the era of e-communication, we cannot ignore the help in e-mailing and downloading the files from internet, and secretarial help in editing the manuscript on computer by Mr B.S. Jadhav, Research Fellow, working on the UGC project in the School. Mr Jadhav took all pains to see that the editing work of the present volume is completed on time. He deserves our heartfelt thanks and appreciations.

Finally, we express our sincere thanks to Mr Pranit Rawat, Rawat Publications, Jaipur for bringing out this volume in record time with commitment.

List of Contributors

Anjali Kulkarni, Faculty Member, Tata Institute of Social Sciences, Rural Campus, P.B. No. 9, Tuljapur, Osmanabad, Maharashtra.

Anjana, Research Scholar, Department of History, Patna University, Patna.

B.C. Barik, Director, School of Social Sciences, S.R.T.M. University, Nanded.

Flavia Agnes, Chairperson, Majlis, Az/4 Golden Valley, Kalina-Kurla Road, Kalina, Mumbai.

Meena Gopal, Reader, Research Centre for Women Studies, S.N.D.T. University, Juhu Campus, Mumbai.

Meena S. Seshu, General Secretary, Sangram, B–11, Akshay Apartments, Chintamani Nagar, Sangli.

Prachi Patwardhan, India Centre for Human Rights and Law, 84, Samuel Street, Dongri, Mumbai.

Priyadershini Pawar, Management Trainee, BAIF Mitra, BAIF Bhavan, Bodle Nagar, Nasik.

Pushpesh Kumar, Faculty Member, School of Social Sciences, S.R.T.M. University, Nanded.

Ratnawali, Faculty Member, Centre for Social Studies, South Gujarat University Campus, Surat.

Renuka Mukadam, India Centre for Human Rights and Law, 84, Samuel Street, Dongri, Mumbai.

Ritambhara Hebbar, Reader, Tata Institute of Social Sciences, Deonar, Mumbai.

Smriti Bhosle, Reader, Department of Sociology, L.J.N.J. College, Vile Parle (E), Mumbai.

Sudarshan Iyengar, Vice-Chancellor, Gujarat Vidyapeeth, Ahmedabad.

Usha S. Sarode, Faculty Member, School of Social Sciences, S.R.T.M. University, Nanded.

Vibhuti Patel, Professor, Department of Economics, S.N.D.T. University, Mumbai.

1

Introduction

Gender and Human Rights: Some Critical Issues

B.C. BARIK, PUSHPESH KUMAR AND USHA S. SARODE

Gender Amidst the Scenario of Concern

We wish to begin this introductory remark by posing a crucial question which most of us in feminist movement might need to ask: "why after centuries of western feminist struggle and several decades of protests in the global south, still we need to articulate women's oppression in contemporary times?" Women's demands have gained considerable legitimacy within the UN and within various national boundaries of developed and developing countries. The governments in developing countries are compellingly verbalizing women's participation in public domains which is now regarded as *crucial* for fulfilling the goals of 'empowerment'. In this scenario of *concern* about women and gender, why do we need to question and critique the very agents who in varying degrees might constitute as actors and partners in feminist transformatory politics? Here, one can see the feminist engagement with state; there are moments of collaboration between the two while there are definite tensions and unease as the state vacillates between progressivism and populism. Feminists have highlighted the contradictory practices of state as far as women's issues are concerned (see Moore, 1988).

Market is a vital player in the globalized world. It has a wider popular acceptance among the middle class which sees it as creating multiple opportunities and opening up newer horizons and avenues of jobs and business. This rather popular belief still persists amidst the recent failure of market to move along with the desire and fantasy of the burgeoning middle class. Against this popular assumptions, why feminist movements should express a word of caution and doubt about the role of market as benefactor? Does it create 'equal' opportunities for all women across the globe? Or, it opens its aperture for some while foreclosing the possibility for majority of poorer women? While women are entering media and entertainment industries in increasing numbers, why we mouth our protest against the 'mainstream' media? While law is changing, with more women friendly laws we have today, why do we still need to cry foul against the legal establishment?

Even if we wear a middle class lance and see the constant symptoms of 'progress' we do need to ask: why the sex ratio is declining in South Asia? Why public places are still unsafe for women? Why the strength of women legislators has not improved much in many countries? Why there is a tacit understanding that there should not be female judges in more numbers in the apex court (Kannabiran, 2005)? Why class and caste still divide our women? Why castes are surging for boundary maintenance in modernizing India with wider proliferation of caste associations in the towns and cities today (cf. Chakravarti, 2003)? Why medical facilities are so unequally distributed? Why hunger and malnutrition still pervades? Why the hypermasculinized male role models are still valorized in identity politics ranging from caste, community to nation (cf. Hansen, 2005)? Why minority women are raped and maimed in India and elsewhere? Why armies rape women of an entire village in places which are rife with ethnic and secessionist conflicts and why all the raped women are subsequently being deserted by their own husbands (cf. Manchanda, 2001)? How the villages where mass rape of women takes place are discursively produced as 'raped villages' within the community and how this heinous act of army is condoned by the state (ibid)? Why honour killings still continue (Welchman and

Hossain, 2006) and how educated and upwardly mobile women are projected in sop operas? They are either vampised or caricaturized. How and why dalit and queer women feel disenchanted with the 'mainstream' women's movement and why they feel the need to 'separately' articulate their own concerns both within and outside women's movement? Why the queer perspective is still not harnessed in developmental rhetoric and why they are also inconspicuous in pedagogical and epistemological practices in South Asia?

Gains are the Outcome of Struggle, not Offered as Charity

We must quickly submit here that whatever legitimate space and visibility women's issues have gained over a period of time is not something in which the state has voluntarily progressed and participated. We do need to salute the hard labour – physical and intellectual – which women of different categories over generations have fought for gender justice. It appears pertinent to bring in here the experiences of a contemporary human right activist Pinar Ilkkaracan[1] who writes: "Well, it might come as a surprise to many – including younger generations of women in the global north, many of whom perceive feminism to be an outdated ideology – that it was only in the early 1990s that the United Nations finally recognized that women and girls also have human rights. If you consider this a bit late in history, you might be even more surprised to learn that the UN did so rather unwillingly, and only under the immense pressure of thousands of women and women's groups both from the south and the north, initiated by a global women's network coordinated by the Center for Women's Global Leadership (CWGL). The network was determined to have women's rights recognized as human rights by the world's governments at the World Conference on Human Rights held in Vienna in 1993, and started to work towards this goal three years before this landmark event".

We need to indulge in these numerous valuable accounts of struggle which women across the globe have waged for their visibility, equality, protection and assertion. Forbes' (1999: 134) accounts of Indian women's movement reveal participation of women of all hues in the nationalist and women's struggle in India – the two cannot really be separated in Indian context. What may shatter our commonsensical belief that women of 'respectable' families have contributed to the nation's and women's cause, is the instance in Forbes' book where she describes how the prostitutes actively contributed for the nationalist cause in the East Godavari district of Andhra Pradesh and Bengal (ibid: 127–28). While talking about revolutionaries in Indian freedom struggle we only salute our male heroes and majority of us have not even heard about the female revolutionaries. Forbes' research brings to light the activities of many revolutionary women. Bina Das, a young college student in Bengal, fired a pistol at Governor Jackson (ibid). Santi and Suniti, two school girls from Comilla, shot magistrate Stevens to death on December 14, 1931 and were the first women martyrs (ibid:140). There were other similar instances which Forbes records in her book. Despite such richness of women activism brought to light by the hard labour of feminist scholars, they are never incorporated in academic and 'nationalist' discourses. She also demonstrates as to how the 'respectable' women participants who came from better off family background abstained from showing solidarity with their 'fallen sisters'.

The more radical (women) activists from the better off background were not welcomed and accommodated by the powerful male nationalist (ibid). This fact is validated in Ray's (2002) account of lives and thoughts of Sarla Devi Chudhrani and Rokeya Shekhawat Hussain[2]. Sarla though concerned with women's cause was a romantic, impressed by traditional domestic Hindu rituals performed in Bengali homes while Rokeya held enormous unease with the helplessness of women of her community. She was almost unique in her bold and direct attack on the precepts of Islam as taught by its guardians, and quite openly ascribed religious texts to male rather than divine origin. It was their particular balance of conformity and non-conformity to dominant views of their times that explain why Sarla secured admiration and support, and Rokeya received a mixed response from her contemporaries (ibid: 98).

These bring us to the whole issue of what a society, a community and or a state expects its women to be? Or, what is regarded as 'proper' for women even in this globalized and liberalized era? Do we still live in a society which fears 'women's freedom' or 'women's assertion' and/or devalues women? We also need to see how women themselves as subjects embody the beliefs and assumptions of society and participate in their own discrimination (see Thapan, 1997; 2007).

Visceral Fear and Anxiety about an Independent Woman

In order to explicate women's position in a given society and at a given period of time one needs to explore and investigate what kind of women society and community wishes for itself and what kind of women they despise and hate and how women respond to these expectations (cf. Uberoi, 2006). It takes us back to the old debate of backlash against a progressive justice during colonial regime in 19th century Maharashtra, where a recalcitrant and resisting wife was despised and opposed by the moralist, conservative and reactionary forces. Ironically, the liberals and reformists also began to see in this brave act of a woman the disruption of old and established Indian tradition and culture (see Chandra,1998).[3] In defeating women's cause, the natives and colonial regime joined hands together and what was witnessed in the process is a reconstitution of patriarchy in colonial India (Sangari and Vaid, 1988). It reminds us of Erndl's (1991: 68) description of fear of female sexuality in Indian culture. She highlights a deep suspicion of women's power and sexuality when unchecked by male control.

Taking recourse to structuralist understanding of society which emphasizes universal underlying logic behind the apparent social forms, we must submit that this visceral fear and anxieties about female sexuality cut across community lines. For example, both Hindu and Muslim communities in India share similar concern for the women who are acting autonomously on their own behalf. The backlash against Shah Bano by conservative Muslim community leaders and Hindu community's sanction and justification of *sati* are cases in point (see Kannabiran, 2005). Indian state which poses itself as the 'protector' of women collaborated with the community in both instances: in one case it compelled Shah Bano to go back to the personal laws when she was seeking justice under secular laws, and in another, it failed to call the *sati* as murder while upholding the right of community (read male) to celebrate the event in the name of culture. Hasan (1994) has pithily explained this collaboration between community and state. To her, in this process of negotiation, the state gives primacy to community and fails to protect an individual woman's rights. State and community not only legitimize patriarchal institutions but they also reproduce and legitimize each other. This mutual legitimacy is forged at the cost of women of the community and women of the nation. Here one can understand the duality and contradictory practices of the state. On the one hand, it may bring in Domestic Violence Act under international pressure and pressures from feminist movements, on the other hand, it will preserve the rights of community to bring reform within itself – a powerful rhetoric in human rights discourse. It is generally known who speaks in the name of the community? The self-determination of the community becomes equivalent to the self-determination of powerful men. Here state fails to intervene in the community on behalf of women. Community as gird of patriarchal power has been aptly described by Iveković and Mostov (2004: 13). They write: "Community is a vertical patriarchal construction claiming a self-referential genealogy in identity and re-configurating one whenever needed. It is hierarchal and non-democratic and does not recognize time. It is a transmission of commands in immediate mode. In a community (and thus within the nation), the communication between individuals is always indirect and goes through a higher office or principle (hegemonic idea or colonizing universals) with some (the hegemonic group) can identify directly, but to which the others can only be subjected. In the sate and nation-building projects, women may be 'liberated' from other, to be dominated from within."

Configuring Gender within Human Rights

The present volume is the outcome of two consecutive national-level seminars on 'Gender and Human Rights' organized in 2004 and 2005 at the School of Social Sciences, Swami Ramanand Teerth Marathwada University, Nanded. The major focus of the present volume is on gendered violence and sex-based discriminations at community level. Voices of women from the margins such as women in prostitution, queer women and tribal women find specific place in essays published in this volume. The first essay by eminent legal feminist Flavia Agnes delineates the dangers of Uniform Civil Code (UCC) debate within a communally vitiated political climate which culminate in demonizing and othering the Muslims while equating Hindus with the nation and also exonerating the latter from all discriminatory practices. Flavia rightly points out that it creates a fiction that Hindus are governed by secular, egalitarian and gender-just family code. She demonstrates how the apex court through its pronouncements ignites UCC controversy and how the mainstream media repeatedly hype it and keep it alive in popular parlance. Her essay interestingly brings home the point that the lump sum provisions for future security awarded by the courts within Islamic principles seemed to be a better safeguard against destitution among divorced women than the secular law. During Shah Bano controversy, the denial of rights of a meagre maintenance dole was lamented by all and sundry notwithstanding the fact that maintenance awarded to the wife of an advocate with a flourishing practice was just 25 rupees in the first instance and 179 rupees in the appeal. Flavia also outlines the plights of Hindu women, particularly from lower socio-economic strata: she demonstrates how certain provisions underlying Section 125 Criminal Proceduce Code (CrPC) are being used by the husbands to defeat the maintenance claim of the former.

Vibhuti Patel's paper dwells upon numerous forms of public and private violence against women in Asia and the Pacific. Her paper is rich both in terms of empirical evidence and feminist analysis. She begins with social paradigm of violence against women which surfaces in patriarchal practices governing the choices that women can make and the resistance they can throw. The forms of violence listed and discussed range from female foeticide and infanticide to unsafe abortion, health risks through occupational and pollution hazards, war crimes, rape brutalization and domestic violence, child sexual abuse, prostitution to culture specific violence and honour killings. She mentions how culture of violence is nurtured through dress code, sex segregation and job segregation etc. The violence against the women of minority community and female headed households are other areas which she has touched upon. Finally, she tries to map out albeit in a limited way the strategies of resistance gearing up particularly in bigger cities through the efforts of women's groups and civil societies.

Renuka Mukadam and Prachi Patwardhan focus upon the issue of sexual harassment at workplace. They briefly outline how the landmark Vishakha judgment made it possible for the issue to be brought within the rubric of 'violation of human rights'. The popular myths and beliefs trivialize these forms of violence and tend to blame the victim while exonerating the violators. It is widely felt that women do not do their assigned work and when they are pulled up for the same, they make false and malicious complaints of sexual harassment at workplace. A powerful myth which envelops the popular psyche is that descent women do not get sexually harassed; only those who are provocatively dressed face harassment. The authors argue that the prevention of sexual harassment at workplace is required urgently because it has a lasting emotional, psychological and physical effects on the women who face it. They bring in statistical data to support their points and find that only a few employers in different states have taken steps to comply with the guidelines while most others have not despite government notifications to the effect of implementing Vishakha judgment.

Women in sex work not only face exploitation and exclusion but they intensely feel the violence of stigmatization. Meena Seshu central concern in her paper is on violent language in describing 'women in prostitution'. She argues that this language needs to be transformed in order to restore subjectivity to these women. Women who participate in prostitution use the term 'women in business' while referring to themselves. Now, the agreed term in some activists' parlance is 'people in prostitution and sex work, (PPS) to include all persons who make money out of sex. This humanizing vocabulary is the outcome of discussions at SANGRAM, an NGO at Sangli in Maharashtra and VAMP, a collective of women in prostitution and sex work. Meena, in her paper, highlights that it is always the anxiety about public health which dominates the way most of the societies deal with commercial sex. The HIV/AIDS epidemic has singled out people-in-prostitution and sex work as carriers and vectors of spread of HIV. Apart from the stigma already attached to their work, society has further marginalized them as core transmitter of HIV infection. It fails to recognize that they are but links in the broad networks of heterosexual transmission of HIV. The role of women in prostitution and sex work in HIV/AIDS prevention is little explored despite the fact that it is now being recognized that these women can be best educators of their male clients.

Meena Gopal's essay explores the location of reproductive and sexual rights within the human rights discourse. She discusses the problems in combining these two sets of rights within human rights discourse. She argues a re-articulation of these rights from the perspective of sexual minorities as she aptly demonstrates that in combining these two the voices of sexual minorities are curbed as they tend to fall beyond the ambit of reproduction and hetronormativity. The dominance of reproductive rights rhetoric has caused the invisibility of an array of people of varying ages and non-conforming sexual practices and leaving many marginalized people (such as lesbian, gay, bisexual and transgender people) outside the framework of human rights protection. In this scenario sexual rights become the claim of only married heterosexual people, especially women.

With empirical data collected on reproductive health of girls and women from Tuljapur and Osmanabad districts of Marathwada region in Maharashtra, Anjali Kulkarni's paper finds out that the adolescent girls have very less access to information on contraceptives and their usage. In case of adult women, sterilization appeared to be the dominant form of birth prevention. Women appeared to be less educated on different alternative forms of contraceptives. She lists out a number of de-motivating factors in use of contraceptives. The powerlessness of many women is reflected in the fact that they are not free to decide for or against sterilization. In majority of cases it is the husband and/ or in-laws who decide for a woman's sterilization. In case if a woman has only daughters, she cannot go for family planning operation even if she does not want another pregnancy. The local health staff have very negative attitude towards the woman whose tubectomy fails and she comes for re-operation. It was found that such women are compelled to offer bribes to the doctors at government hospitals. A woman in the initial phase neglects her illness and her husband is the final decision-maker in her seeking treatment. Though treatment efforts start from less expensive sources, the women do not find government sources useful. Kulkarni further notes that there are wide prevalence of health complaints like painful menstruation, heavy discharge, uterus prolapse, STIs, anaemia, etc., but as the health staff have the pressure of completing targets of tubectomy, the women with other health complaints are perceived as 'extra work'.

Smriti Bhosle outlines the rights of female prisoners under trial under various Acts and within the Criminal Manual issued by Bombay High Court (1960). While examining the implementation of these legal provisions among the undertrial women prisoners of Central Prison in Mumbai, Bhosle finds that these women prisoners are deprived to access most of these provisions. She talks about the isolation, insecurity, emotional imbalance and forced separation from the families which these women are faced with. At the end, she suggests women certain measures to ensure human dignity to undertrial prisoners.

Priyadershini Pawar focuses on domestic violence which according to her cuts across caste, class and religious boundaries. She dwells upon the strategies adopted by Family Counselling Centres (FCCs) to deal with cases of domestic violence. It is a countrywide initiative taken by the Central Social Welfare Board (CSWB), New Delhi, through the State Social Welfare Advisory

Board (SSWAB). She provides empirical evidence from FCCs attached to Satara Police Station in western Maharashtra.

The last three essays talk about rights of tribal women within the community. Ritambhara Hebbar finds it very ironical that the Ho community that has been a victim of human rights violation by the state with their women being the equal participants in the community's struggle against injustices are reticent in addressing the issues of gender rights within the community. She emphatically attempts to dispel the myth and imagined fear of the Ho community that granting land rights to women will threaten the patrilineage and subsequently destabilize the families. At a conceptual realm she pithily brings out the whole conflict between cultural rights and individual rights. The rights of a community to practise its culture trivializes the inalienable and indivisible character of human rights guaranteed to every individual. Similar concerns have been expressed in Anjana's paper on customary practices and rights of tribal women. She argues that customary practices among the tribal communities are not necessarily detrimental to the interest of women. There are many customs and norms which provide liberatory space to tribal women while there are others which systematically subjugate them. Taking a diachronic perspective, the paper deals with the changes occurring in customary practices of several tribal communities in India during colonial and post-colonial times in which the state has played a vital role. It is noted that while modifying the customary practices, the colonial and post-colonial states have been generally guided by political expediencies and their own conscious, unconscious ethnocentric assumptions. These have had the potential to erode 'progressive' and liberatory elements of a culture while reinforcing and introducing certain retrograde elements at the detriment of tribal women.

Ratnawali and Sudarshan Iyengar, in their paper, critically analyse the role of state in providing basic health facilities to the tribal women. According to them, Gujarat is one of the progressive states in India. If one looks through the lens of health indicators, the achievement of the state is not satisfactory. The performance is highly skewed and abysmal so far as tribal population in the state is concerned. Till date, the tribal women depend upon traditional 'Dhais' for deliveries and local Bhagats (traditional tribal healers) for cure of other types of diseases. If this is the situation today, how one can expect that the tribal women should fight for their reproductive health rights?

In the end, we hope that the present volume will generate discourse on the issues of gender and human rights, which is of vital social concern today.

Notes

1. Pinar Ilkkaracan is the Founding President of Women for Women's Human Rights, a leading women's advocacy organization in Turkey, and co-founder of The Coalition for Sexual and Bodily Rights in Muslim Societies, an international network of NGOs and academicians working towards promotion of sexual and bodily rights in the Middle East/North Africa and South/Southeast Asia. She has participated in various UN meetings and conferences on women's human rights both as a member of the Turkish delegation and NGO representative. She has written extensively on women and law, sexuality and religion, sexual and reproductive rights, human rights education, and violence against women. She is the editor of *Women and Sexuality in Muslim Societies* (translated into Arabic and Turkish) and *Deconstructing Sexuality in the Middle East and North Africa: Contemporary Issues and Discourses*.
2. We bring in here the cases of these two women to emphasize that radical women are even now being resented within and outside feminist movement which is narrated by several feminist activists in the metropolitan India. It gives the impression that patriarchal culture has not altered radically despite considerable changes sweeping in as a result of liberalization and globalization. In popular perception, radical women are looked as home breakers. Sarla who epitomized woman activist balancing Hindu traditionalism belonged to Hindu-Brahmo community. She was related to Tagores, unquestionably the most illustrious family in Bengal. Rokeya Shekhawat Hussain came from a traditional Muslim zamindar family from northern Bengal. Though Rokeya was a supporter of anti-colonial struggle her prime concern was gender justice – the colonization of women's mind by men (see Ray, 2002 for further details).
3. This is concerned with the famous case of Rukmabai in late 19th century Maharashtra. Rukmabai's reluctance to join her husband through the consummation of marriage triggered off a social drama

when her husband Dadaji Bhikhaji filed a case against her in the Bombay High Court in 1884. The drama reached its peak in 1885, when Justice Pinhey, in a historical verdict, declined to pass a decree of restitution of conjugal rights in favour of the husband. The revivalist and conservative forces interpreted this judgment as an interference in the sacrosanct arena of Hindu conjugality by British courts. This led to a flurry of protest ultimately defeating the cause of a woman. A woman's subversive moves are similarly checked time to time by community power or by the patriarchal practices operating through different formal informal institutions. See Chandra (1988) and Flavia Agnes in this volume.

References

Chakravarti, Uma. 2003. *Gendering Caste through Feminist Lens.* Kolkata: Stree.

Chandra, Sudhir. 1998. *Enslaved Daughters: Colonialism, Law and Women's Rights.* Delhi: Oxford University Press.

Erndl, Kathleen M. 1994. 'The Mutilation of *Surpnakha*'. *In* Paula Richman (ed.) *Many Rayamanas: The Diversity of Narrative Tradition in South Asia.* pp. 67–88. Delhi: Oxford University Press.

Forbes, Geraldine. 1999. *Women in Modern India.* UK: Cambridge University Press.

Hansen, Thomas Blom. 2005. 'Sovereigns Beyond the State'. *In* Ravinder Kaur (ed.) *Religion, Violence and Political Mobilization in South Asia.* New Delhi: Sage Publications.

Hasan, Zoya. 1994. 'Contextualising Gender and Identity in Contemporary India'. *In* Zoya Hassan (ed.) *Forging Identities: Gender Community and State.* New Delhi: Kali for Women.

Iveković, Rada and Julie Mostov. 2004. *From Gender to Nation.* New Delhi: Kali for Women.

Kannabiran, Kalpana. 2005. *The Violence of Normal Times.* Delhi: Women Unlimited.

Manchanda, Rita. 2001. 'Guns and *Burqa*: Women in Kashmir Conflict' *In* Rita Manchanda (ed.) *Women, War and Peace in South Asia.* New Delhi: Sage Publications. pp. 42–101.

Moore, Henrietta. 1988. *Feminism and Anthropology.* London: Polity Press.

Ray, Bharati. 2002. *Early Feminists of Colonial India: Sarla Devi Chaudhurani and Rokeya Sakhawat Hossain*. Delhi: Oxford University Press.

Sangari, Kumkum and Sudesh Vaid. 1989. 'Recasting Women: An Introduction'. *In* Kumkum Sangari and Sudesh Vaid (ed.) *Recasting Women: Essays in Colonial History*. Delhi: Kali for Women.

Thapan, Meenakshi (ed.) 1997. 'Gender and Embodiment in Everyday Life'. *Embodiment: Essays on Gender and Identity*. New Delhi: Oxford University Press.

—, 2007. 'Adolescence, Embodiment and Gender Identity: Elite Women in Changing Society'. *In* Rehana Ghadially (ed.) *Urban Women in Contemporary India: A Reader*. New Delhi: Sage Publications.

Uberoi, Patricia. 2006. *Freedom and Destiny: Gender, Family and Popular Culture in India*. Delhi: Oxford University Press.

Welchman, Lynn and Sara Hossain. 2005. Introduction: 'Honour': Rights and Wrongs. *In* Lynn Welchman and Sara Hossain (ed.) *'Honour': Crimes, Paradigms, and Violence Against Women*. Delhi: Zubaan.

2

Dominant Ideologies and Gender Concerns

A Fresh Look at the Uniform Civil Code Debate

FLAVIA AGNES

The Supreme Court, the Media and the UCC Debate

Periodical pronouncements by the Supreme Court, urging the state to enact a Uniform Civil Code (UCC), have received wide media publicity. The myriad opinions expressed in support of the UCC are governed by three distinct undertones, i.e., gender equality, national integration and concept of modernity embedded within the notion of middle class morality.

The gender concerns project the demand for an all-encompassing uniform code as a magic wand, which will ameliorate the woes and sufferings of Indian women in general and Muslim women in particular. This concern places gender as a neutral terrain, distanced from contemporary political processes. From this point of view, the agency for change within communities becomes highly suspect. Minority women are projected as lacking a voice and an agency either in their own communities or through the process of litigation to claim their rights within existing structures. It projects the state intervention in the form of an enactment of a uniform code as the only option to bestow gender justice upon minority women.

At another level, for the liberal, modern, English educated, middle classes, the demand is laden with a moral undertone of abolishing polygamy and other 'barbaric' customs of the minorities and extending to them the egalitarian code of the 'enlightened majority'. This position relies upon the western model of nation-state and liberal democracy and scorns simultaneous sexual relationships in the nature of polygamous marriages in the name of modernity but, at the same time, endorses sequential plurality of sexual relationships (through frequent divorces), and also the more recent trends of informal cohabitations which have gained legitimacy in the West.

Within a communally vitiated political climate, the demand also voices concerns of 'national integration' and 'communal harmony' and projects Muslims as the 'other' both of Hindus and the nation. At times the distinction between these two terms collapses and they become interchangeable.

It is indeed a matter of grave concern that this position, advocated by the Hindu right wing, received a boost through judgments pronounced by the Supreme Court of a secular and pluralistic state, and more often than not by the presiding Chief Justices. It is interesting to note that no matter what the core issue litigated before the apex court, the comments regarding the enactment of a UCC are always made in reference to 'national integration' and either a veiled or direct insinuation against Muslim law, thus creating a fiction that Hindus are governed by secular, egalitarian and gender just family code and it was high time that this code was extended to Muslims to usher in modernity and gender equality among them. This communal posture of the apex court becomes evident when we examine the constitutional challenges to archaic and sexist provisions of Hindu law. For instance, when in 1984, the Delhi High Court[1] upheld the archaic provision of restitution of conjugal rights under the Hindu Marriage Act which was challenged on the basis that it violates freedom and equality, not only was there no mention of a UCC and 'national integration' but the court went further and ruled: "Introduction of constitutional law in the home is most inappropriate. It is like pushing a bull into a china shop. It will prove to be a ruthless destroyer of the marriage institution and all that it stands for. In the privacy of the home and married life, neither Article 21 nor Article 14 have any place." This decision was later affirmed by the Supreme Court.[2]

While the blame for igniting the UCC controversy must lie primarily with the Supreme Court, the blame for repeatedly fanning it and keeping it alive in popular parlance lies with the media. While the Shah Bano judgment[3] provided the first impetus for highlighting the polarized opinions into mutually exclusive segments – the progressive-modernist in support of a UCC and fundamentalist-obscurantist in opposition, it has continued to frame the issue within these binaries even when the lines between these two sections have become blurred. In the two decades since the Shah Bano ruling the ground realities have changed substantially. The demolition of the Babri Masjid, the rise of the Hindu right wing, the attacks on Christians, and the gruesome sexual violence upon Muslim women during the recent Gujarat carnage have all been factors that have necessitated a re-examination of the earlier call for a UCC, ostensibly to secure the rights of minority women. Many progressive groups and some women's organizations no longer support this demand.

What is even more relevant is that the BJP, the dominant segment of the ruling National Democratic Alliance (NDA) itself, has abandoned it, though this was one of the its major election planks (along with the Mandir at Ayodhya and abolition of Article 370 – a cultural *thrishul* – a three-pronged attack against Muslims). In fact, during the last elections, the demand for a UCC was been dropped from the common NDA election manifesto.

Despite this, the polarization in the media continues and the same old controversy gets whipped up again and again and is savoured with relish by the English-speaking urban, liberal, middle class. And, this class, which is otherwise indifferent to political processes, becomes the ardent defender of the demand for the UCC. Every time the Supreme Court makes a comment, what one sees in the media are images of *purdah*-clad Muslim women and opinions of Muslim religious leaders opposing the demand. Many times, the core issues litigated before the Supreme Court are blotted out and the call for a UCC is projected as a pronouncement against the Muslim minority.

For instance, the judgment pronounced by Chief Justice V. N. Khare in the John Vallamattom's case in August 2003 concerned a Christian priest's personal freedom to make a bequest of religious-charitable nature. But a stray and uncalled for comment regarding the UCC helped the media to convert a judgment in defence of personal freedoms and cultural plurality into one in defence of UCC and hence, anti-minority. Ironically, the next day and through the weeks that followed, the newspapers were flooded with reports and editorials on UCC with quotes from Muslim religious leadership and intelligentsia on one end and women's rights activists on the other, while the judgment itself was of relevant neither to the Muslim identity nor women's rights.

Similarly, in the *Sarla Mudgal* case,[4] the core issue before the court was conversion and bigamy by Hindu men. Here again, neither Muslim law nor rights of Muslim women were issues before the court. The court was examining the rights of two Hindu wives and the validity of two marriages by a bigamous Hindu husband – the prior one under the Hindu law and the subsequent one contracted after a fraudulent conversion to Islam. Despite this, the parties to the litigation were all Hindus and continued to be so. But, unfortunately, the judgment and the media publicity that followed focussed primarily on UCC in the context of nation, national integration and minority identity. Of the three judgments, the Shah Bano alone had an aggrieved Muslim woman at its core. And, this controversy warrants a re-evaluation in the light of subsequent developments.

Revisiting Shah Bano and the Controversial Muslim Women's Act

The facts of the Shah Bano judgment, which first raised the controversy of a Uniform Civil Code (UCC), are now history. It would suffice to mention that the Supreme Court elected to comment upon Islam and the Muslim Personal Law while deciding the right of maintenance under a secular and uniform statute. But this was not the first instance of the apex court upholding the right of the divorce Muslim woman for maintenance. Two significant decisions of the Supreme Court delivered by Justice Krishna Iyer in 1979 and 1980 in *Bai Tahira*[5] and *Fuzlununbi*[6] respectively had placed the divorced Muslim woman's right of maintenance under this provision upon a secure footing without arousing a political controversy.

The unwarranted comments evoked a communal backlash. Relenting to the pressure exerted by the Muslim orthodoxy, the government introduced the Muslim Women's Bill which sought to exclude divorced Muslim women from the purview of Section 125 of Criminal Procedure Code (CrPC). This move by the ruling Congress, led by Rajiv Gandhi, came to be projected as the most glaring instance of the defeat of the principle of gender justice for the Indian women as well as the defeat of secular principles within the Indian polity.

This move met with severe opposition from secular and women's rights groups. As the debate progressed, the media projected two insular and mutually exclusive positions, i.e., those who opposed the bill and supported the demand for a UCC as modern, secular and rational, and those opposing the UCC as fundamentalist, orthodox, male chauvinist, communal and obscurantist. To be progressive, modern and secular was also to be nationalist and conversely the opposing faction could be labelled as anti-national. As the controversy escalated, the Muslim was defined as the other, both of the nation and of the Hindus. Muslims, in turn, could be mobilized to view this as yet another threat to their tenuous security. The rigid approach of the Muslim leadership provided further fuel to the Hindu right wing forces in their anti-Muslim propaganda.

Ironically, the fury which was whipped up, seemed to be divorced from the core component of the controversy, a paltry sum of Rs.179 per month, far too inadequate to save the 73-year old ex-wife of a successful Kanpur-based lawyer, from vagrancy and penury. The raging controversy and the communal turn of events finally led Shah Bano herself to make a public declaration renouncing her claim, strengthening the popular misconception that Islam subverts economic rights of women. If this entitlement was against her religion, she declared, she would rather be a devout Muslim than claim her right of maintenance. A sad comment indeed, warranting reflection from campaigners on both sides of the divide. The statute, passed under a party whip, led to a further strengthening of the Muslim appeasement theory in judicial discourse and in popular media.

The hurriedly drafted and hastily enacted statute was full of loopholes. But, despite its limitations, the Act was of immense historical significance, as the first attempt of independent India, to codify the Muslim Personal Law. But, the positions across the divide were so rigid by then, that they left no space to contemplate upon this milestone. It is only when the dust raised by the controversy settled down that one could examine the relevance of this statute titled, Muslim Women's (Protection of Rights on Divorce) Act, 1986 (MWA). But since it was enacted amidst protests from women's rights groups and progressive social organizations, it was viewed with suspicion and foreboding by these sections. Hence, the first response of the protesting groups was to challenge its constitutionality, rather than examine its viability.

While the writ petitions filed by various organizations were pending in the Supreme Court, the Act gradually unfolded itself in the lower courts. Appeals from the decisions of various High Courts gradually started accumulating, along with the original writ petitions. What was intriguing was that while the writ petitions were filed by groups agitating for women's rights, the appeals were from husbands aggrieved by the verdicts of various High Courts. If indeed the Act was depriving women of their rights and was enabling husbands to wriggle out of their economic liability, why were the husbands finding themselves aggrieved by the orders passed under a blatantly anti-women statute? Lurking beneath was a faint suspicion that perhaps the manner in which the Act was unfolding itself in the lower courts, was indicative of a different reality, defying the premonitions. This fascinating phenomenon provided the first indication that perhaps the ill-famed Act could be invoked to secure the rights of divorced Muslim women.

A seemingly innocuous clause, which had missed the attention of protesters and defenders alike, had been invoked by a section of the lower judiciary, to pronounce judgments, which provided greater scope for protection against destitution. Section 3 (1)(a) of the Act stipulated that a divorced Muslim woman is entitled to a reasonable and fair provision and maintenance to be made and paid to her within the *iddat* period by her former husband. This clause, along with the preamble "An Act to protect the rights of Muslim women who have been divorced by, or have obtained divorce from their husbands ....", had been invoked by the judiciary in defence of Muslim women's rights.

Though initially just a trickle, the judgments were a pointer towards a possibility. They affirmed that the new Act was to protect the rights of divorced Muslim women and not deprive them of their rights. They further stressed that any ambiguity within the Act must be interpreted in such a manner as to reconcile with the proclamation contained in the title of the Act. Banishing divorced women to a life of destitution would not amount to protecting their rights as stipulated by the statute, they declared.

Suddenly, the lump sum provisions for future security, which the courts were awarding within the framework of Islamic principles, seemed to be a better safeguard against destitution, than the meagre doles which they were entitled to under Section 125 of CrPC . A reading of the judgments indicates that the Act had rid itself of the agenda of alleviating vagrancy and destitution among divorced women and had extended itself to the claims of women from a higher social strata. The statute enacted in haste, at the insistence of the conservative leadership, seemed to have boomeranged. A concerned and sensitive judiciary carved out a space for the protection of women's rights from what appeared to be an erroneously conceived, badly formulated and blatantly discriminatory statute, without invoking a political backlash. Drawing on the Islamic concept of *mataaoon bil ma'aroofe* (fair and reasonable provision), the courts opened a new portal for the protection of divorced Muslim women.

The ruling of the five-judge constitutional bench, headed by Justice G.B. Pattanaik in *Daniel Latifi*[7], pronounced on 28th September 2001 by a five judge bench, finally put its seal of approval on these positive interpretations.

Muslim Women, Dominant Ideologies and the Media

Law is not merely a statute; its essence lies in the manner in which it is unfolded in law courts. The empty words of a statute come to life in trial courts where they are contested, interpreted and validated. Right from 1988, the courts have engineered divorced Muslim women's rights through innovative interpretations of the Muslim Women's Act, ushering in a new set of rights within the established principles of Muslim law. Several judges declared that 'provision' contemplates 'future needs' and that the parliament has replaced one set of obligations of a Muslim husband with another. The claim under the Muslim Women's Act does not operate through a rider of sexual purity. The judicial pronouncements delivered divorced Muslim women from the cumbersome burden of recurring monthly dues, which hinged upon post-divorce chastity.

But rather unfortunately, within the communally vitiated atmosphere, the advances made by divorced Muslim women under MWA have been invisibilized and glossed over by the media. During the Shah Bano controversy, the denial of rights of a meagre maintenance dole was lamented by all and sundry, notwithstanding the fact that the maintenance awarded to the wife of an advocate with a flourishing practice was just Rs.25 in the first instance and Rs.179 in appeal. So long as the debate could be used as a stick to beat the community with, these minor details did not seem to matter. What did matter is the fact that a communal campaign could be mounted upon a patriarchal paradigm and thereby legitimized.

The demand for a UCC was couched as a 'liberal and modernizing mission'. The irony lay in the fact that the groundwork for mounting this campaign was laid by the women's movement, with genuine gender concerns, but firmly located within the cultural ethos of the mainstream. Within this framework, a similar appeasement of Hindus, by strengthening coparcenaries by various legislative measures, could be deliberately ignored. The 'modernizing mission' is an important tool for establishing racial and communal superiority and is used constantly by dominant classes and hegemonic cultures. During the colonial rule, the introduction of the Anglo-Saxon legal structure was seen by the

British administrators as an important forte of its civilizing mission and that the Hindu society could rid itself of its barbarism and enter an era of 'civilization' through it. An image of the cruel and superstitious native who needed Christian salvation was deliberately constructed by the Evangelists. In post-independent India a similar framework is being used to justify the barbarities against the minority communities through the dominant ideology.

One needs to examine the invisibilizing of the Muslim women's struggle within the cultural construct of these hegemonic claims. The communal fervour could be sustained only by denying the fact that the Act provided for an alternate remedy, far superior to the one that had been denied to Muslim women under Section 125 of CrPC; by negating the fact that since 1988, the Act was being positively interpreted by various High Courts in the country by awarding substantial amounts as 'settlements'; by glossing over an important development in the realm of family law, that of determination of economic entitlements upon divorce, rather than the prevailing right of recurring maintenance. So, even while homes of poor Muslim women were looted, gutted and razed to the ground in various communal riots, while teenage sons of Muslim women were killed at point blank ranges in police firings, while Muslim women were raped under flood lights in post-Babri Masjid riots, the mainstream continued to lament over *Muslim appeasement* and denial of maintenance to *poor Muslim women /the Shah Banos*.

One could overlook even this. Perhaps there was a justification. Denial of maintenance by husbands was perhaps as loathsome as rape of women in communal riots. In the ultimate analysis, it was the poor Muslim woman who suffered. So far so good. But how can one logically explain the recurring motif of Muslim appeasement even after the Supreme Court decision when the controversy was finally laid to rest by upholding the constitutional validity of the Act and simultaneously securing for the Muslim women maintenance rights which in actual terms are superior to the rights bestowed upon a Hindu woman?

And yet, the rhetoric continues. And is used yet again, in defence of the Gujarat carnage. "They had it coming ... they have been 'appeased' beyond tolerance. Why should they demand a separate law in a secular country? Why should they be allowed to marry four times? Why are Hindus alone bound by an obligation of maintenance?" What is startling is that the grievances are mouthed not only by Hindu extremists but also by centrists, the liberals, the people who inhabit my social space, the urban, cosmopolitan, middle class. Within the cultural ethos of the mainstream, an injustice to a Muslim wife gets magically transformed into a Hindu injury which could be invoked to justify communal carnage. Without this tacit approval by the middle class, the recent Gujarat carnage could never have spread so wide nor so deep.

The rhetoric conveniently overlooks the fact that abandonment and destitution of wives is as rampant among Hindus; that the matrimonial faults of adultery and bigamy are evenly distributed across communities; and that Hindus, Christians and Parsees, with equal zeal, guard the patriarchal prerogatives within their respective personal laws. Further, that around 80 per cent of all women burnt in their matrimonial homes are urban middle class Hindus! That patriarchal prerogatives cannot be abandoned even when a law is being codified is something we have learnt in the process of Hindu law reforms. Even when codification is sought in the name of either 'uniformity', 'national integration' or as a 'civilizing mission', these prerogatives will be retained. The saving of Hindu undivided family (HUF) property under the Hindu Succession Act is a glaring example of this. The Hindu urban and rural propertied class and family business establishments have gained the maximum concessions of tax benefits due to this. Any move to abolish this even under the guise of a UCC will be opposed vehemently by this class, as it will upset their apple cart. For them, the UCC debate is confined to abolishing the 'barbaric' Muslim culture of polygamy and to liberate the Shah Banos, while simultaneously turning a blind eye to the sexual promiscuity and multiple sexual relations among them. The women bound in these relations can easily be discarded as 'concubines', 'mistresses' or partners of contractual agreements, *maitreyee karars* (this is the modern term for these alliances) lacking legal validity and devoid of any rights, as one experiences during contested claims of maintenance by these women.

Viewed within this background, the struggles of individual divorced Muslim women who defied their culture and tradition and dictates of patriarchy have to be acknowledged as acts of assertion. Divorced Muslim women had to fight every inch of the way for their rights right from the trial courts in small district towns up to the Supreme Court. Their crucial right of survival hinged upon interpretations and explanations of simple words like 'within/for' 'and/or' 'maintenance/provision', disjunctures and conjuctures of words and phrases.

In the final battle in the Supreme Court, both sides, the women's rights groups who had challenged the constitutionality of the Act as well as the Muslim religious leadership who had pressed for their claim that the Muslim woman's entitlement ought to be limited to three months of *iddat* period, lost out. Who emerged victorious was the divorced Muslim woman who had waged a relentless battle to defend her rights. It is now time the media took note of this silent revolution waged by individual Muslim women and acknowledge the fact of their agency in bringing about changes within their personal laws.

Monogamy, Morality and Maintenance

In this concluding part, I would like to contextualize sexual morality and its co-relationship to claims of maintenance. I have mentioned earlier that the claim under the Muslim Women's Act does not operate through a rider of sexual purity. It would indeed be interesting to explore how this co-relationship between sexual purity and maintenance claim is played out in court rooms. Within the Indian family law, women's economic claims arising out of a marriage contract are confined to recurring monthly maintenance. It is only under the Muslim Women's Act, the principle of determining economic rights upon divorce has been introduced in the Indian matrimonial jurisprudence.

A large number of deserted Hindu women, particularly from the lower strata, find it more convenient to claim this right under Section 125 of CrPC rather than under the Hindu Marriage Act, as the proceedings under Section 125 are summary and are situated in the proximate magistrate's court than the distant district court (except where family courts have been set up). This otherwise innocuous section, came alive through the Shah Bano controversy in 1985 and is retained in public memory due to the furor it caused at the time. But, the notions of sexual morality with which this section is governed has not received due attention in contemporary feminist legal discourse.

The stipulation under clauses 4 and 5 of this section that a woman who is living in adultery is not entitled to maintenance, provides the armour for husbands to entangle women in vicious and dilatory litigation over a pittance of maintenance. A careful scrutiny of reported cases in any law journal would reveal the extent to allegations of sexual promiscuity are made to subvert women's claims. To give an example, a journal widely used by lawyers practising matrimonial law *Divorce and Matrimonial Cases* (DMC) for 2001 reports around 45 cases under the title "Maintenance". In almost half of these, sexuality and morality were the core issues which were contested. An important point to note is that from litigation in the magistrate's court, the cases went through cumbersome processes to the higher courts for them to merit a reporting in the law journal. Hence, they reflect only a tip of the iceberg. In each of these cases the women were assaulted and driven out. Most of these cases also contained allegations of dowry harassment. But none of these women had filed a criminal complaint under Section 498A of IPC. All they did was to file an application for maintenance and it is then that the husbands lashed out with allegations of sexual promiscuity.

The layered and multiple contexts through which sexual morality surfaces, as per the norms of patriarchy, serve only one end – to challenge the legitimacy of women's claims. It is a clear case of "heads I win and tails you lose." The allegations ranged from adultery on the part of the wife and disputing paternity of the child to allegations of a subsisting previous marriage of the wife, husband's subsisting first marriage, allegations of concubinage and husband's subsequent marriage. But, the issues of sexuality, morality and polygamy, whichever way they emerge, can always be turned against the woman's claims of maintenance. For instance, it really does not matter whether the woman's previous marriage or the husband's previous marriage is in dispute. So long as sexuality is pitted against maintenance claims, it is the woman who has to pay the price.

Scanning through the judgments one can see a positive trend emerging, where the courts have upheld the women's claims and disallowed the husbands' contentions. But, despite this, the prevalence of Section 125 (4) and (5) provides the scope for the husbands to entangle the deserted women from the lower strata, in prolonged, cumbersome and costly litigations. And, negative rulings, though less frequent, still prevail. A judgment of the Allahabad High Court[8] is quoted here to convey to the readers the extent of humiliation a woman goes through during these litigations: "If the man and woman choose to live together and indulge into sex no such marriage status can be conferred automatically by their so living upon such a woman. She is not entitled to the legal status of a wife in the eyes of law and society. Law and society treat such women either as concubine or a mistress ... The two may agree to live together to satisfy their animal needs. But such a union is never called a marriage. A woman leading such a life cannot be bestowed with the sacrosanct honour of wife. No marital obligations accrue to such a woman against her husband. Such a wife must be termed as an adulterous."

One measure which is being suggested to resolve the ambiguity of a Hindu marriage is compulsory registration of marriages. This rigid stance of morality would lead to placing all Hindu marriages in a straightjacket and invalidating all unregistered marriages. This will only serve to make the situation worse for women of this category. This would indeed be regressive and deprive them of the presumption of marriage due to prolonged cohabitation, and the presumption of legitimacy of children which is presently available under the India an Evidence Act.

The positive trend found in some recent suggestion for reforms is to validate the rights of second wives/cohabitants. For instance, the Malimath Commission report has suggested that the term 'wife' under Section 125 of CrPC should include "a woman who was living with the man like his wife for reasonable long period". Though the report has several anti-women recommendations, this particular positive one needs to be highlighted.

Even more relevant is the provision in the proposed Civil Law on Domestic Violence. This bill, initially drafted by activists groups, takes the issue even beyond and seeks to grant rights of residence to cohabitants and women in informal relationships and protect such women from domestic violence. This provision was endorsed by the Parliamentary Standing Committee on Human Resource Development, in its 124th report, in the following words: "The Committee is aware of the fact that in our society there are numerous cases where a man and a woman, though not legally married, live together as husband and wife ... The Committee, therefore, suggests that the Bill should be suitably amended to include those women also who have been living in relationship akin to marriages and in marriages considered invalid by law".

While these are welcome trends, how do we connect them to the debate on UCC which is mounted on the plank of monogamy? It is not my intention here to hold a brief for sexual promiscuity of either men or women – be they Hindu, Muslim or even Christian or Parsee. All I wish to do is to raise an uncomfortable question: when de-linked from rights of maintenance and residence, would the claim for monogamy still survive as a plank for the UCC discourse. Or even further, whether concepts of gender equality, national integration and sexual morality are artificially superimposed upon the UCC discourse by vested communal interests and whether, in the context of recent developments, the binaries in which the debate is located have become redundant. And even more daunting is the question: what innovative measures are needed to protect the crucial economic rights of women within the family and in informal sexual relationships, even beyond their right of residence and maintenance and the confines of personal laws.

HINDU CONJUGALITY: HISTORIC AND CONTEMPORARY DEVELOPMENTS

A Tribute to Rukhmabai

In January 2004, at a solemn function, graced by the Chief Justice of India and the legal luminaries of the country, the magnificent and monumental edifice of the Bombay High Court building celebrated its 125th anniversary. While eulogies were paid to the great traditions of this High Court, an issue that went unnoticed was the role this High Court had played in framing, moulding and defending women's rights. Hence, perhaps, it is apt to start this essay by paying tribute to the herculean battles waged by individual women before this mighty 'High Court of Judicature at Bombay' in defence of their right to basic human dignity.

Of particular importance is the struggle of a young woman, Rukhmabai, who defied tradition and the colonial legal dictates by refusing to be bound to a marriage contracted when she was barely eleven. The social drama, which unfolded around her legal case has been described as a unique event in colonial India by some historians. Her legal battle can easily be termed as one of the glorious events played out in the theatre of a great court. Questioning what was assumed to be natural, she offered a subversive model of assertion by women of their desire, as individuals, in a terrain dominated by family, community, and imperial notions of justice and governance.

The social drama was triggered off when Dadaji Bhikaji filed a case against Rukhmabai in the Bombay High Court in 1884.[9] It reached its peak in 1885, when Justice Pinhey, in a historical verdict, declined to pass a decree of restitution of conjugal rights in favour of the husband. In a bold and fearless verdict, he declared that since conjugality had not been instituted, the question of granting the relief of 'restoring conjugality' did not apply to this case. The Judge proclaimed:

> "It is a misnomer to call this 'a suit for the restitution of conjugal rights'. Restitution of conjugal rights can only apply to a situation when a married couple, after cohabitation, separate and live apart. Here, the husband has asked the court to compel the wife to go to his house, so that he may complete his contract with her by consummating the marriage. It seems to me that it would be a barbarous, cruel and revolting thing to do, to compel a young lady under those circumstances to go to a man whom she dislikes, in order that he may cohabit with her against her will. No law or practice justifies such an order. I am not obliged to grant the plaintiff the relief which he seeks, and to compel this young lady of twenty two to go to the house of her husband in order that he may consummate the marriage arranged for her during her helpless infancy. .... the practice of allowing suits for the restitution of conjugal rights originated in England under peculiar circumstances,

> and was transplanted from England into India. It has no foundation in Hindu law ... For many years after I came to India such suits were not allowed. It is only of late years the practice of allowing such suits has been introduced into this country from England (I think only since the amalgamation of the old Supreme and Sadar Courts in the present High Courts which has brought English lawyers more into contact with the mofussil). It is, in my opinion, a matter for regret that the remedy of restitution of conjugal rights was ever introduced into this country".

Ironically, the revivalists interpreted this judgment as an interference in the sacrosanct arena of Hindu conjugality by the British courts (and a breach of the assurance on non-interference). For the reformers the intervention of the English courts was an armour in their campaign against the upper caste Hindu custom of child marriage.

The litigation, the judgment and the controversy which followed were all laden with ironies. The husband's case was trumpeted by the revivalists and it is with their support he had approached the English courts, rather than the caste panchayat, for the remedy of restoring his Hindu conjugality. Within the customary law, the relief of restoring conjugality was non-existent and the husband could not obtain any relief in this sphere. Also, the parties belonged to the lower caste among whom the custom of the caste recognized the right of the wife to dissolve her marriage. And, most important, Justice Pinhey had declined the relief on the ground that it was an outdated medieval Christian remedy under the English law and further that the Hindu law did not recognize such a barbaric custom!

But, in the highly politicized climate, these subtle legal points were lost. And, within this politically surcharged atmosphere, the husband filed an appeal. And, the colonial courts succumbed to the political pressure. In 1886, the division bench presided over by Chief Justice Sir Charles Sargent and Justice Bayley rejected the argument that there is no authority for a decree for 'institution' of conjugal rights under Hindu law and decreed: "The gist of the action for restitution of conjugal rights is that married persons are bound to live together. Whether the withdrawal is before or after consummation, there has been a violation of conjugal duty which entitles the injured party to the relief prayed." The court ruled in favour of the husband and granted him the decree of 'restitution of conjugal rights'.

But how was this decree to be enforced? The civil courts did not have the power to bodily reinstate conjugality – a power which the European ecclesiastical (church) courts had. Hence, the only way the decree could be enforced was through civil imprisonment and attachment of property. In a moment of pride and glory for Indian women for centuries to come, Rukhmabai declared that she would willingly undergo imprisonment rather than let a man she detested enforce conjugality!

If the court was compelled to execute its own order, it would indeed have been a matter of blemish for the colonial rulers, who had justified their rule on the premise of ushering in modernity and defending women's rights. The then prevailing prisons, in their primitive conditions, did not even have the provision to imprison a woman, let alone a woman of Rukhmabai's stature. Fortunately, for all concerned, the matter was finally 'settled' by payment of compensation by Rukhmabai to her husband.

Rukhmabai struggle is relevant not only for its times but even for the contemporary international women's rights discourse. The motif of Rukhmabai's defiance of both, the verdict of the alien English judges and the patriarchal dictates crouched in national pride, in defence of her right over her personhood, at a time when English women were waging a battle for their right to own separate property as wives, would indeed serve to shift the rigid and fixed binaries of First World feminists/Third World victims.

Restoring Hindu Conjugality in Modern Times

It is interesting to explore how the concept of restitution of conjugal rights, which Judge Pinhey of the Bombay High Court had described as an "archaic Christian remedy of medieval Europe" in 1885 while adjudicating over the Rukhmabai case, has been played out in modern times under the codified Hindu law.

The codified Hindu Marriage Act of 1955 is based on a formal concept of equality. The spouses are deemed to be equally placed and are deemed to have equal rights and obligations towards each other. This concept did not exist under any prevalent legal system. The Hindu law, either scriptural or customary, or the Muslim law or even in the modern and secular Special Marriage Act, enacted in 1954, did not recognize this concept. It was introduced for the first time under the Hindu Marriage Act and was based on the western notion of formal equality.

So, while a basic inequality between men and women persisted within the scheme of inheritance rights (by the retention of the HUF property through which a male gets a share in the family property by birth) under the perverse logic of equality, the Hindu woman was placed under a legal obligation to maintain her husband. While an 18-year-old boy is not entitled to claim maintenance from his father on the ground that he had reached the age of majority and hence is capable of earning his own livelihood, an adult male is granted the privilege of exercising a choice of remaining unemployed and claiming maintenance from his employed wife.

Ironically, while women were burdened with the responsibility of maintaining the husband under a modern concept of equality, the courts continued to undermine a woman's right to retain her job against her husband's wishes under the ancient notion of 'Lord and Master' and granted him the privilege of determining the choice of matrimonial home. If the woman was employed at a place away from the matrimonial home, the husband could claim restitution of conjugal rights against her.

For decades after the enactment, in a series of decisions, the courts held that Hindu marriage is a sacrament and it is the sacred duty of the wife to follow her husband and reside with him wherever he chooses to reside. In all the cases the women were working and supporting the family. The husbands had approached the courts for restoring conjugality just to spite the women. The courts upheld the husband's rights and granted them a decree of restitution.

In 1958, in *Ram Prakash v Savitri Devi,*[10] the Punjab High Court held: "According to Hindu law, marriage is a holy union for the performance of marital duties with her husband where he may choose to reside and to fulfil her duties in her husband's home." In 1964, in *Tirath Kaur v Kirpal Singh,*[11] the wife pleaded that she was willing to carry on with the marriage but was not prepared to give up the job. The court disallowed her plea and ruled in favour of the husband on the ground that the wife's refusal to give up the job amounts to desertion. In 1966 the Madhya Pradesh High Court held: "A wife's first duty to her husband is to submit herself obediently to his authority and to remain under his roof and protection." In 1973, in *Surinder Kaur v Gardeep Singh*[12] it was held: "The Hindu law imposes on the wife the duty of attendance, obedience to and veneration for the husband to live with him wherever he chooses to reside."

The leading judgment on this issue came in 1977, in the case of *Kailash Wati v Ayodhia Parkash.*[13] The wife was employed prior to the marriage. Seven years after the marriage, the husband asked the wife to resign her job and on her refusal to do so, filed for restitution of conjugal rights. The wife stated that she was prepared to honour her matrimonial obligations but was not prepared to resign her job. The full bench of Punjab and Haryana High Court held: "According to Hindu law, marriage is a holy union for the performance of marital duties with her husband where he may choose to reside and to fulfil her duties in her husband's home." The court reaffirmed that the wife's refusal to resign her job amounts to withdrawal from the husband's society, and granted the decree in favour of the husband.

So, while under the modern concept of equality, the husbands had the right to be maintained by their wives, under the ancient concept of a sacramental marriage, they could restrain them from gainful employment. While the husbands' plea that it is the sacred duty of a Hindu wife to reside under his 'care and protection' is not surprising, the judicial affirmation of this plea under a modern statute is disturbing.

It is only around 1975, two decades after the enactment of the Hindu Marriage Act, that the courts began to recognize the woman's right to hold on to a job away from her husband's residence. In a significant ruling, the Gujarat High Court, while denying the husband the relief declared: "In the modern outlook, the husband and wife are equally free to take up a job and retain it. Since there had been a mutual arrangement, it was not a case where it could be said that the wife had withdrawn from the society of the husband."

The significant ruling on this issue came from the Delhi High Court in 1978, in *Swaraj Garg v R.M. Garg.*[14] Dissenting from the full bench decision in *Kailash Wati* the court held that in the absence of a pre-marital agreement between the parties, it cannot be said that the wife who had a permanent job with good income had to live at a place determined by the husband when the husband did not earn enough to maintain the family.

But, despite this ruling, the practice of filing a suit for restitution of conjugal rights by husbands for maintenance continues. In a study of family courts in Maharashtra and Karnataka, conducted by the author for the concerned State Commissions, it was revealed that husbands file disproportionately higher cases of restitution of conjugal rights as compared to any other matrimonial relief. The judges presiding over the family courts comment that it is an usual practice adopted by lawyers defending husbands, to file a suit for restitution of conjugal rights to defeat the women's claim for maintenance.

But the vagaries of law are strange indeed. In recent time, applying innovative legal strategies, some women's rights lawyers have been able to use this blatantly anti-women provision to protect women's right to marriage and matrimonial home.

Apex Court and Hindu Conjugality

A public debate on restitution of conjugal rights (RCR) will remain incomplete without a discussion on its constitutionality. Two High Courts and the Supreme Court examined this issue in early eighties. The pendulum swung from one end to the other and finally settled to augment the masculine power and authority.

The first among these was the judgment of Justice P.A. Choudhury in 1983. The case concerned the marriage of a screen actress, T. Sareetha,[15] who had left her matrimonial home. Her husband Venkatasubbiah tried to curb her freedom by filing a suit for RCR and obtained a favourable order. But, like Rukhmabai, a century earlier, Sareetha stood firm in her decision. Instead of complying with the court order, she filed an appeal in the Andhra Pradesh High Court.

It was then that Justice Choudhury delivered the historical judgment and held that the remedy is savage and barbaric. He struck down the concerned section and redeemed Sareetha and all women of Andhra Pradesh, from the oppressive yoke of Hindu conjugality. In a clear and unambiguous voice he proclaimed: "The remedy of restitution of conjugal rights is violative of the right to privacy and human dignity guaranteed by Article 21 of the Constitution. A decree of restitution of conjugal rights constitutes the grossest form of violation of an individual's right to privacy. It denies woman her choice whether, when and how, her body is to become the vehicle for the procreation of another human being. It does not promote any legitimate public purpose based on any concept of social good."

With extreme sensitivity, Justice Choudhury addressed the male privilege of marital rape latent in the RCR provision. His is one of the earliest judicial voices which challenged the superficial gender neutrality of the Hindu Marriage Act. He declared: "It appears that Section 9 of the Hindu Marriage Act does not offend the principle of equality, since it does not discriminate between a husband and wife. On the other hand, by making the remedy equally available both to wife and husband, it apparently satisfies the equality test. But bare equality of treatment, regardless of the inequality of realities, is neither justice nor homage to the Constitutional principles."

His is also one of the earliest voices which declared that women's rights are human rights by bringing them within the ambit of Article 21 of the Constitution and by extending the scope of 'right to life' to include right to human dignity of women. But his stand had no takers. Rather unfortunately for Hindu women, the respite granted by Justice Choudhury was short-lived. In the following year, the Delhi High Court examined the same issue and held to the contrary. This judgment makes interesting reading.

The wife, Harvinder Kaur,[16] had challenged the decree of RCR granted in favour of her husband Harmender Singh, by the lower court. The Delhi High Court dismissed her appeal and upheld the husband's right to restore conjugality and declared that Section 9 of the Hindu Marriage Act is constitutionally valid. The court further explained: "The object of a decree of RCR is to bring about cohabitation between the estranged parties so that they can live together in amity. It is a two in-one provision. On the one hand, it enables the court to coax and cajole the parties to resume marital life and is designed to encourage reconciliation."

The court then went even further and provided a perverse logic for its explanation: "Introduction of constitutional law in home is most inappropriate. It is like introducing a bull in a china shop. It will prove to be a ruthless destroyer of the marriage institution. In the privacy of the home neither Article 21 nor Article 14 have any place. In a sensitive sphere which is most intimate and delicate, the introduction of the cold principles of constitutional law will have the effect of weakening the marriage bond. The introduction of constitutional law into the ordinary domestic relationship of husband and wife will strike at its very root and will be a fruitful source of dissent and quarrelling. The 'domestic community' does not rest on contracts sealed with seals and sealing wax, nor on constitutional law. It rests on that kind of moral cement which unites and produces 'two-in-oneship'."

If only this opinion was not so tragic for women, perhaps one might have appreciated it as a judicial comedy. The controversy created by these two diagonally opposite viewpoints was reconciled by the Supreme Court ... by overruling the verdict of the Andhra Pradesh High Court!

The case before the court is illustrative of the manner in which the provision works for women. When her husband had deserted her, Saroj Rani[17] approached the court for a decree of RCR. Her husband, Sudarshan Kumar, did not contest and a decree of RCR and Saroj Rani obtained a decree in her favour. In the following year, Sudarshan filed for divorce under Section 13 (A) of the Hindu Marriage Act on the ground that one year had passed since the passing of the decree and no cohabitation had taken place between them. The wife submitted that when she had gone to the matrimonial home to 'restore conjugality', she had been thrown out. Based on this, the trial court dismissed the husband's petition. But in appeal he succeeded. The wife approached the Supreme Court for setting aside the divorce decree passed by the High Court on the ground that the husband cannot be permitted to take advantage of his own wrong. On her behalf it was argued that Indian wives should not be made to suffer at the hands of manipulative and dishonest husbands.

But, the apex court dismissed her appeal, upheld the divorce granted by the High Court and held: "Non-compliance of the decree of RCR does not amount to 'taking advantage of his or her own wrong'. Though we cannot rule out the possibility of a party obtaining a decree and then not enforcing the same with the sole purpose of getting a divorce after the lapse of statutory period, such abuse can be prevented only by bringing in changes in the legislation to plug the misuse. But as the law stands now, we are helpless."

In the process, the court also examined the constitutional validity of the provision and held: "In India, conjugal rights, i.e. right of the husband or the wife to the society of the other spouse is not only a creation of the statute. Such a right is inherent in the very institution of marriage itself. There are sufficient safeguards in Section 9 to prevent it from being a tyranny. It is significant to note that the decree can be executed by attachment of property. A decree of RCR offers inducement for the husband or wife to live together. It serves a social purpose as an aid to the prevention of break-up of marriage."

It appears that the judges inhabit a different social space than us – the lesser mortals. So, the provision continues and can be used by the husbands in two different ways. When the wife files for maintenance, RCR proceedings are initiated to deny her maintenance. If a deserted wife files for RCR, the husband can consent to a decree in wife's favour and then prevent the wife's re-entry into the matrimonial home. After the lapse of the statutory period of one year, he can get a divorce without the necessity of having to prove any other matrimonial offence. This is how 'equality' works under the Hindu Marriage Act and the sacred Hindu conjugality is legally preserved with the benevolence of the apex court!

"Bend It Like Beckham"

In this exploration on Hindu conjugality, I have taken the readers from the historic Rukhmabai case, through the myriad ways in which the courts augmented masculine power and authority and throttled women's rights on the pretext that the remedy of restitution of conjugal rights induces reconciliation and prevents break-up of marriages. In this concluding part, I will take the readers from the revered plane of legal academics to the messy arena of litigation and explore whether and in what manner, this outdated and anti-women provision can be used to protect women's rights.

The approach adopted by some lawyers, while dealing with women's dispossession from the matrimonial home, can best be explained by borrowing the popular phrase, *Bend it like Beckham*. Activists believe that rights are located in law and lay a great emphasis in statutory reforms. But, in the realm of matrimonial laws which are based on the principle of equality, every legal provision introduced to protect women, can also be used against them. It is innovative strategies that clinch the issue for women. The approach that has helped me while defending women's rights has been to accept that litigation is a game of chess. If that be so, then it has to be played with the same legal acumen and precision, as a chess champion would approach a game of chess.

Borrowing again from the saying, a "bird in the hand is worth two in the bush" a pro-active approach is worth a hundred defensive strategies. More often than not defensive strategies would only amount to 'crying over spilt milk'. Illustrative of this is the case of Seema who approached us in a shattered state when she was thrown out of the matrimonial home. Her's was an inter-community 'love marriage' to a man from a higher social strata. After seven years, love had flown out of the window and Seema was subjected to battering and constant threats. The cause was the husband's involvement with a young woman from his own community. This usual story might have ended in the usual way, with Seema losing all her rights when she was thrown out of the matrimonial home. But things worked out differently for her.

Fearing arrest in the event that Seema filed a police complaint, the husband absconded with her five-year-old son and left the matrimonial home vacant. Seema had been a home-maker, having given up her job on her husband's insistence. Though homelessness and poverty stared her in the face, like most women in her condition, her immediate concern was only to get back her son. But claiming custody when the woman is thrown out of the matrimonial home, is not as easy as it seems. Despite the legal provisions favouring women, judges usually adopt the approach of 'maintain *status quo*' as far as children are concerned. The courts are generally not inclined to change the established custody order and disturb the child at the interim stage. So, rather than tamely accepting her fate, our advice to her was to take a pro-active and aggressive litigation stance. Since the locked premises constitute her matrimonial home, we convinced her that she has every right to break open the lock, and enter the matrimonial home and it would not amount to 'housebreaking'. If she was in the house, how long could the husband stay away?

The strategy worked like magic. Initially, when Seema approached the local police and was denied police protection, she was scared. It took quite a bit of cajoling to get her to agree to our suggestion of breaking the lock. The next day we were in court with a suit for restitution of conjugal rights and obtained an ad-interim order of injunction restraining the husband from dispossessing her! When this was served on the husband at his parental place, to say the least, he was shocked. That the frail and forlorn Seema could bring him to his knees in an aggressively strategized litigation was not something he had bargained for. We also obtained a second order – to produce the child in court within a week.

The child, who had been separated from the mother for nearly a month, clung to her during access and that clinched the issue of interim custody. We also got an injunction restraining the husband from removing the child from her custody. The fourth order secured Seema's right to the exclusive use of a bedroom and part of the kitchen. Later, she was awarded three thousand rupees by way of maintenance to her and the child. By now, Seema was secure having protected her rights over both home and child and a reasonably good order for maintenance to take care of her daily expenses. This helped to transform Seema into a self-confident and assertive person. When her husband filed for divorce in another court, she was in a position to dictate her terms. The matter was finally resolved with the husband buying a separate apartment for Seema and the litigation ended with a decree of divorce by mutual consent.

Not every case turns out to be as great a success story as Seema's. But right to matrimonial residence is becoming an important component of matrimonial litigation for women, who are battered and are routinely dispossessed and rendered shelterless. A women's rights lawyer cannot afford to ignore this reality. The women's need for a safe shelter is turning the tone and texture of matrimonial litigation in metropolitan cities. The remedy is becoming even more crucial for women than the conventional remedies of divorce or maintenance. In a country which has failed to enact a legislation for women's right to matrimonial home and property, some lawyers have taken the aid of the anti-women remedy of restitution of conjugal rights, as a means of overcoming the legislative void. This is a circuitous way of obtaining a basic and fundamental right of dignity, security and survival. But faced with a legal vacuum, women's rights lawyers are forced to adopt aggressive and innovative strategies to save women from destitution and deprivation. A civil remedy of injunction or a subsidiary relief in a suit for restitution of conjugal rights are the slender threads upon which women's right against dispossession from the matrimonial home hinges.

The recently formulated Domestic Violence Act has tried to address this issue and has introduced the concept of matrimonial residence but rather stealthily, without initiating a public debate. When the bill was presented in Parliament, to the dismay of women's groups, this remedy was glaringly missing. Later the Parliament was dissolved, the bill itself had lapsed. While the protective orders in a domestic violence situation are important, the issue of matrimonial residence and property needs to be foregrounded as a campaign issue in its own right and public awareness needs to be generated to secure this crucial right of survival. Unless this is done, merely deleting the provision of restitution of conjugal rights may not be the best solution to the problem faced by women.

To sum up, the remedy of restitution of conjugal rights has, both historically and contemporarily, been a volatile litigation arena, used by husbands to subordinate women to sexual claims of conjugality. By conceding to these claims, the courts have legitimized martial rape. It has also been used to defeat maintenance claims or throttle rights of gainful employment or as a means of surreptiously obtaining divorce as in the case of Saroj Rani discussed earlier. More recently, through innovative legal interventions, a few women like Seema have been able to secure their right of matrimonial residence through this. But whichever way one examines the issue, the remedy is far removed from the judicial notions that it facilitates reconciliation, brings in matrimonial harmony and prevents the break down of marriages! While adjudicating over women's rights, our judges need to examine the letter of law in the context of the socio-economic situation in which the litigation is grounded!

Notes

1. *Harvinder Kaur v Harmander Singh* , AIR 1984 Del 66.
2. AIR 1984 SC 562.
3. AIR 1985 S C 945.
4. (1995) 3 SCC 635.
5. AIR 1979 SC 362.
6. AIR 1980 SC 1730.
7. 2001 CriLJ 4660.
8. I (2001) DMC 313 (All).
9. (1886) 10 BOM 301.
10. AIR 1958 PUNJ 87.
11. AIR 1964 PUNJ 28.
12. AIR 1973 P & H 134.
13. ILR (1977) 1 P&H 642.
14. AIR 1978 DELHI 296.
15. AIR 1983 A.P. 356.
16. AIR 1984 DELHI 66.
17. AIR 1984 SC 1562.

3

Growing Violence Against Women

Issues and Strategies

VIBHUTI PATEL

Violence against women (VAW) has become a central issue in the discourses of the international women's movement in the 21st century. Women's networks in the Asia-Pacific region have taken up wide range of issues concerning VAW in their personal lives as well as against the systems perpetuating it. "Personal is political" – a slogan popularized by two decades of women's movement in the last century – signifies consistent campaigns against all forms of violence in women's intimate/personal and public/societal lives. The Asia-Pacific region is experiencing wide range of violence against women at different stages of their lives, from womb to tomb, as a result of modernization and commercialization of subsistence economies, family ties becoming less supportive, increasing migration, demanding work (shift from *just-in-case* approach to *just-in-time* approach of the production processes) and also due to rising fundamentalism.

During the eighties, women's rights organizations mushroomed in the Asia-Pacific region and focussed their attention on VAW. They organized rallies and demonstrations, sit-ins and conventions, seminars and conferences, which culminated into politics of protest movements and petitioning. In the 1990s, the women's groups consolidated their base by finding their allies in the state apparatus and created their institutional base and shelter homes for women and children victims of violence.

It is therefore important to understand, analyse and combat octopussy clutches of VAW to ensure right to dignified life to womenfolk of our country.

Social Paradigms

Let us first examine the social paradigms associated with VAW. Women's status in the family is determined by *panchmahabhoota* (five omnipresent factors) of patriarchy, namely, caste/kinship network, religion, economic status, media and the state policies. It draws its strength from male dominance and female subordination. Life cycle of a woman is governed by value system, which promotes preferential treatment for men and neglect of women. Antenatal sex-determination tests, female infanticide, neglect of daughter in terms of food, health care and educational facilities and personality development result into stunted growth of women. Discrimination and violence faced by women, from womb to tomb, make women suffer from the sense of low self-esteem and psychological dependence.

Violence Against Women in Asia and Pacific in the New Millennium—A Collage

The following poem by Lara Jesani aptly captures the gravity of VAW in different covert and overt forms:

Battered Woman

Someone in the crowd of a hundred
is a badly battered woman.

Someone in the crowd of a hundred
is a widely relishing man
Even if you don't believe this theory
You are supposed to know,
Every second of an hour

A woman is battered sore.
Some women in the crowd of a hundred
Are killed as soon as they are born

No one cares for her future
For her life is only torn.

You might not believe me surely
You might as well be informed
A man is given more importance
Than women when they are born.

One woman in the crowd of a hundred
Is respected when she is at birth
Only one man in the crowd of a hundred
Takes a woman out of deep dirt.

You don't need to believe what I say
But you must surely be shown
How for a ninety-nine women
The future of one man is glowed.

One woman in the crowd of a hundred
Is not a victim of this injustice
But all men in the crowd of a hundred
The honour of women in all ways dismiss.

Female infanticides and female foeticides in India and China have created adverse juvenile sex ratio. Historical legacy of strong son preference and neglect of daughters has taken a dangerous turn where scientific technologies for sex determination, such as amniocentesis, chorion-villi-biopsy, foetoscopy, sonography, are abused for selective abortion of female foetuses by money-minded medical professionals (Patel, 2002, 2003, 2004). Sex-selective abortions of female foetuses accounted for 17.6 per cent of 1,492 induced abortions in a sample survey in India (Ganatara, Hirve and Rao, 2001). New reproductive technologies of pre-selection of unborn babies prevent birth of girl child. Several Asian countries have declining sex ratio, i.e., number of women as compared to 1,000 men is less than 1,000. Noble laureate, Prof Amartya Sen calls this phenomenon 'missing women' (Sen, 1992). This is a manifestation of discrimination and stigmatization of women delivering daughters. "Sex selection in society occurs in the context of entrenched values, interests and cultural beliefs and practices. Their eradication requires investment in long-term strategies and economic and social development and educational and cultural empowerment" (Chee, 2002). It is a matter of deep regret that even the states in Asia perceive this phenomenon as an indicator of population stabilization – logic being less number of women means less reproduction. In the language of demography, it is called Net Reproduction Rate of 1 (NRR1), which means mother is replaced by one daughter (Karkal, 1991).

Abortion in Asia-Pacific Countries

Criminalization of abortion in Nepal renders thousands of girls and women into prisons. "Both, the woman who undergoes the procedure and the service provider can be imprisoned" (Shrestha, Tamang and Sharma, 2001). Abortion laws in several Asian countries victimize the victims, especially innocent adolescent girls, who have no control over their sexuality and fertility. Teenage pregnancy is a major issue for the civil societies in the rural Asia, still no attention is paid by the states to safeguard the interests of girls. Chances of a woman dying from complications of pregnancy or childbirth during her lifetime are 1 in 65 in Asia (WHO, 1996). Majority of abortions in Asia are unsafe and are performed by unauthorized practitioners. Recently, a multi-centric study involving seven states of India by CEHAT, Mumbai also proves this point.

Economic Development and VAW

Women from the Asia-Pacific region are supposed to be relatively timid, obedient, disciplined and meticulous to handle skilled, monotonous jobs, and easy to control. New international division of labour, intensified by globalization, depends on super-exploitation of poor Asian women, especially young unmarried girls, who are recruited in the Free Trade Zones (FTZs), Export Processing Zones (EPZs) and the latest, Special Economic Zones (SEZs). During the last two decades, in the absence of any democratic rights in these labour concentration camps, these young girls had only one way of expressing their anger, fatigue and alienation, i.e., mass hysteria (AWRAN, 1985). Now, the heads of ASEAN countries are negotiating to create more and more EPZs, SEZs and FTZs. Human and women's rights groups need to ensure that the horrible past of back-breaking, hazardous, highly labour-intensive workload for women workers in the region is not repeated.

Industrial pollution and occupational health risks also take heavy toll of Asian women's reproductive health. Carcinogenic and mutogenic effects of industrial pollution, mercury poisoning of fisherfolks of Minamata in Japan, Union Carbide gas tragedy in Bhopal (India) Jelly Fish babies in Fiji Islands as a result of dumping of nuclear waste have raised danger signals. Commercialization of forest and natural resources has enhanced rural women's plight, as they are responsible for collection of fuel, fodder and water.

The modernization project in the Asia-Pacific region is connected with racist and sexist biases of population control policies that dump burden of population control on women. Targeting of poor Bangladeshi or Malay women for forced sterilization and Indian or Indonesian women for unsafe hormone-based contraceptives and pro-natalist policy for educated Asian women in a bid to enhance the quality of population are two sides of the same coin. We must highlight sexist implications of Eugenics. All these efforts violate bodily integrity of women and rest on the presumption that penetrative sex is be-all and end-all of women's existence. After the introduction of Structural Adjustment Programmes (SAPs), states in the region have reduced social sector budget for women's development that comprise health and nutrition, education, employment and empowerment. Two categories for which the states are pumping in massive amount of funds are population control programmes and military expenditure.

Globalization and VAW: New Forms

In the absence of any safety net provided by the multinational and transnational corporations or the governments, globalization has enhanced control over sexuality, fertility and labour of women migrants in the region. Innocent rural girls as well as high-school educated adolescent girls are inducted into the workforce. Cross-country migration of girls and women for domestic work, industrial and professional work and services like nursing, secretarial practice, tele-calling has increased.

'Mail-order brides' from Asian countries are in demand in Europe so that ageing patriarchs can be looked after by 'docile' Asian women. Organ trade of destitute women, children and foetuses from the poor Asian communities has gained demonic proportion. Soft porn as well as hard-core pornography and cyber sexual violence are used for terrorization, humiliation and intimidation of women and girls (Shin, 2002). Cyber stalking in the computer labs of offices, colleges, universities and commercially-run-cyber-cafes has invited attention of the decision-makers who are divided in their opinions (Hitchcock, 2002). Some scholars believe that it reduces actual VAW as people derive psychological satisfaction through voyeurism. Others see it as an extension of verbal and physical violence. Policy interventions are needed to deal with online sexual violence (Chang, 2002). Use of SMS to send scary messages to girls, is another important area that demands urgent attention (Herring, 2002). Only the East Asian countries have addressed cyber violence with gendered perspective (Lee, 2002). In cities like Mumbai, Delhi, Bangalore, Chandigarh and Hyderabad, increasing number of women are reporting harassment by online sexual violence through spam mail, cyber porn and SMS messages.

Smut parties for executives of TNCs, MNCs and indigenous corporate barons have become routine affairs, so much so that the states in the region do not take any action in spite of prima-facie evidences provided by the newspaper coverage (Shyam, 2002).

Jingoism, Militarization and VAW in Asia

Implications of jingoism – psychology of war mongering are – dire on Asian women. Politics of rape used against women in Kashmir conflict, the tragedy of Tamil women in conflict, insurgency in Nepal, refugee camps, conflicts in Indo-China have evoked extreme indignation from the human rights organizations all over the world (Manchanda, 2001). In Myanmar, the military rulers use rape as a means of social control and use torture for women deemed dangerous to the regime. Jingoism in South Asia has enhanced insecurity for women in the border regions of the sub-continent. Women's groups of SAARC countries have demanded peace and have launched several programmes for public awareness.

'Comfort women' of militarymen from World War II to Vietnam war have approached the UN system for justice. Drugs, sex shops and crimes connected with militarization in Indo-China are reminders of medieval barbarism. Women as carriers for smuggling, women in border regions and women in the refugee camps of conflict-ridden areas need civilian interventions for safety and security. In region constituting 'killing fields' in Kampuchea women constitute two-thirds of population. Development programmes supported by the UN are inadequate. International NGOs need to take lead in this direction. Mass rape of women in the East Timore by Indonesian soldiers, who are also owners of brothels, needs to be condemned by the international community. Institutionalization of sex slavery in the region demands collective efforts of women's networks in the region.

Domestic Violence

Mapping of domestic violence in the region reveals universality of its occurrence still, "health data collected routinely by governments and WHO do not yet report on the incidence of violence against women. For Asia-Pacific region, country prevalence studies show that the prevalence of violence by an intimate partner ranges between 16 and 40 per cent" (Abdullah, 2002). Domestic abuse is everywhere in Vietnam, still, there is no shelter-home for women. In most Asian countries, there is no legal or state provision against marital rape (Poonanchit-Korsieporn, 2000).

A team of Bombay Municipal Corporation (BMC) doctors, women activists and researchers visited crisis centres in hospitals in Philippines and Malaysia in 1999. Inspired by this study tour, they facilitated the process of replicating the hospital-based crisis intervention centre and invited Centre for Enquiry into Health and Allied Themes (CEHAT) to set up one stop crisis centre for women, called Dilaasa, in collaboration with BMC-run Bhabha Hospital, Mumbai (Jesani, 2002).

How to Prevent Child Sexual Abuse?

Increasing incidences of child sexual abuse are reported in the region, mostly by street children and child labourers. Hence counselling of children in school is not adequate. There is need for community and neighbourhood-centred approach. We also need public discussion, TV coverage, radio talks to legitimize experiences of the victims and empower them. Code of conduct concerning adult-child relationship, do's and don'ts and unsafe touch/intimacy should be discussed openly, not in a hush-hush tone. We should teach our children that "It is O.K. to say 'No' ", instead of unconditional obedience. We should organize assertiveness training sessions and create a non-threatening atmosphere for children to emphasize, "Speak out, don't suffer in silence". Docudrama and role play for classroom teaching should highlight all potential situations of child sexual abuse. Custodial situations – hostels, jails, mental hospitals, orphanages, shelter homes and family – need special mention. Accountability, transparency, responsible media coverage are imperative on part of the criminal justice system. Visually effective posters showing safe alternatives to abusive conditions should be addressed to school-going and non-school-going children. Ban on use of children for child pornography should be made effective in the region. Sleazy remixes of old songs are making obscene use of women's bodies.

Prostitution

Sex tourism in South and South East Asia perpetuates and promotes child prostitution. In Myanmar, every year, 10,000 women and girls are trafficked into sex slavery in Thai brothels. Same is the profile of rural girls in India, Nepal, Bangladesh, Sri Lanka in South Asia, Thailand, Philippines, Indonesia and Malaysia and in Indo-China. Both worsening economic situation and cultural practices condoning multiple sex partners are responsible for proliferation of prostitution. HIV/AIDS scare has had no effect in curbing sex trade in the absence of economically viable alternatives for sex workers.

Laws concerning prevention and suppression of trafficking in women and children should ensure de-criminalization of victims of prostitution targeting 4 Ps – procurers, pimps, police, politicians. Dealing with blackmailers needs support of the community groups and civil society initiatives. State funding for rehabilitation of prostitutes and salary of frontline workers should be increased so that better quality of custodial care and developmental needs of ex-prostitutes in terms of education, skills, employment, healthy recreational activities can be provided. Close collaboration between GOs and NGOs can be most effective (Fernandes and Ray, 2002). They should encourage analytical, not sensational, writings or media coverage on prostitution.

HIV/AIDS as a Worst Form of VAW

This is a very important issue being raised in the 21st century. Both sex workers with multiple sex partners and housewives with single sex partner (i.e., husband) are at risk of getting HIV/AIDS. Counselling for dealing with social stigma and creating an alternate support network are the most important aspects of providing emotional support to the HIV/AIDS patients. The Lawyers' Collective HIV/AIDS Unit holds monthly drop-in meetings, with an objective of sharing information, experiences and resolving mind-boggling issues affecting the lives of HIV/AIDS patients. It also provides legal aid and allied services to the needy. "The main objective of the Unit is to protect and promote the fundamental rights of persons living with HIV/AIDS who have been denied their rights in areas such as health care, employment, terminal dues like gratuity, pension, marital rights relating to maintenance, custody of children and housing" (Lawyers' Collective, 2000).

Culture-Specific VAW

Culture-specific violence against women in different Asian and Pacific countries should be dealt with sensitively, without making any racist or chauvinist remarks against the concerned communities. We need universal applicability of human rights and treat women's rights also as human rights. We should keep this in mind while dealing with cases pertaining to culture-specific violence against women, e.g., *sati* in India.

Valourization of Barbaric Behaviour with Women of Minority Communities

In the riots after breaking of Babri mosque, the use of video cameras to capture the glory details of the rape of Muslim women in Surat, in the presence of military and para-military forces, revealed the most horrific dimensions of brutalization of the psyche of the civil society. Showing of these video films in front of jeering crowd left permanent scar in the minds of women and children of minority communities. Their sense of shame was complete. Even in Somalia, the fundamentalist forces used the videotapes women showing weeping and wailing naked violated rape victim to terrorize, humiliate and intimidate women and to show them their place of restricted existence. Cleansing operations in Bhopal (1992) and Gujarat riots (2002 onwards) have created nightmarish situation for the Muslim women who experienced worst forms of sexual violence – rape, torture and tearing of uterus of pregnant women (Engineer, 2003). While rape is a crime perpetrated during communal conflicts, the use of media to record, duplicate and even sell videos of rape is unprecedented and speaks of the dangerous use of media. Apart from this, the insular feelings created after each riot result into confinement and restriction of mobility of women and girls.

The nation-states in all parts of the globe have proved to be ruthlessly against the minorities. In England, when temples and mosques are demolished by all types of chauvinist forces (Hindus, Muslims and Skinheads), state machinery chooses not to address these issues on the grounds of non-interference with minorities. The policy of 'multiculturalism' in Britain and 'respect for all religions' in India should be seen in this light. Patriarchal bias of the state always compromises women's interests so that the ruling party can fetch block votes by pleasing the patriarchs of the minority/migrant communities. Non-interference by the state when adult girls are confined by their family members so that they do not run away with their boy friends and can be hurriedly forced into arranged marriage, is part of this game.

Fundamentalism, Communalism and VAW

Denial of human rights and fundamental rights enshrined in the Constitution of India by the fundamentalists by imposition of dress code, not granting right to work and attacks on female-headed households have been objected by women's rights groups throughout the world. Extreme form of punishment meted to women by the fundamentalists is in the form of stoning to death of 'an adulterous woman' by the assembled community. During the last decade innumerable women in several countries have lost their lives in painful and undignified manner at the hands of self-appointed 'custodians of morality'. 'Honour killing' has become most widespread among all types of fundamentalists and communalists throughout Asia, Africa and the Middle East, not only among the tribals, but also among the so-called civilized sections of the nation-states. Recently, the law court of Shariat in Nigeria has passed a judgment of stoning to death to a mother of an infant, Amina Lowal, for adultery. There has been an international uproar against the judgment. As a result, for the first time, the state has not executed the decision of the Shariat.

Sex segregation: The fundamentalists forces have prevailed upon the state to enforce sex segregation in Iran, Albania, Sahel in West Africa, Pakhtun, Malaysia and Turkey (Hjarpe, 1983). "Women in Saudi Arabia live complex existence which mingles strict traditions and codes of conduct with modern demands of education and freedom" (Megalli, 2002). Non-entry of women in the stadium and sports complexes practised in several theocratic states. On 22 January 2003, the Chief Justice of Afghanistan ordered nationwide ban on cable television and co-education (WLUML, 2003).

In December 2002, Al Badr Mujahideen and Lashkar-e-Jabbar, offshoots of Lashkar-e-Toiba pasted a poster outside a Government Higher Secondary School, in Afghanistan asking girls to discontinue their studies.

Dress code: Kashmir conflict has created a situation of great fear and insecurity in women's lives (Dewan, 2002). Those who opposed the imposition of burqa by Kashmiri militants had to face dire consequences. Under the Taliban rule, Afghanistan went to absurd lengths to implement Islamic laws that made women's life a never-ending punishment. It imposed ban on drivers of all types of vehicles from carrying women not wearing *chador* or *chadri*. It also prevented women from washing their linen in rivers and deserts (Pevrin, 1997). In India too, a senior Shiv Sena leader, Nanak Ram Thavani has urged the federal and state governments to formulate and implement a dress code for girls in all schools, colleges and other teaching institutes (WLUML, 2003).

Within hours of the expiry of their deadline for Muslim women and girls to wear burqa, the Kashmiri fundamentalist militants killed three women, including two students and a teacher on the morning of 20th December, 2002 at Hasiyot in Thanamandi tehsil of Rajouri district *(The Indian Express, 27* December 2002).

Right to work: Women were the first targets of theocratic states in both the neo-colonial and post-liberation phases in the Middle Eastern, the Mediterranean and the North-West Frontier countries. In all these countries, women bravely fought along with their male comrades against the imperialist forces. But once, the "revolution" or the "national liberation" was attained, the fundamentalist forces dumped women into the four walls of domesticity. *Arab News*, the Saudi English language daily, has revealed that Saudi women are more concerned about finding good work in tough jobs than being veiled.

The Kashmiri militant group, Lashkar-e-Jabbar has asked Muslim women to quit their jobs and stay home, or face punishment, including death (*The Times of India,* 21 January 2003).

In spite of the threats by the fundamentalists women are entering male bastions such as foreign services, diplomatic missions, judiciary, military, police force, sports such as soccer, political bodies, academic institutions, industrial chambers even in the theocratic states.

Female-headed households: Fundamentalists of all hues perceive female-headed households as an eye sore and make all efforts to persecute, stigmatize, isolate, marginalize and terrorize deserted, divorced, single and separated women for leading an independent, economically self-sufficient life with dependent children or senior citizens. They do not accept women as heads of the household. Wherever the fundamentalist forces have become powerful, the female-headed households face persecution and witch-hunting.

Communalized education: In the Tenth National Conference of the Indian Association of Women's Studies the issue of communalization of school and college textbooks was discussed at length as representatives of different states reported that there was "a systematic attempt by the Sangh Parivar to 'educate' young and old through schools, shakhas, temple networks, *satsangs,* etc. Through such education, which encompasses a whole range of institutions, the Sangh Parivar has managed to draw into its fold large number of women, who in turn seem to transmit this hatred to their children" (IAWS, 2003).

Changes in the curriculum that is being pushed through the National Curriculum Framework and the new NCERT textbooks portray women only in highly regressive patriarchal terms within the framework of the family. They have targeted women's movement as being responsible for the break up of the family. Many women's studies scholars have interpreted Gujarat tragedy as a failure of education that created brutalised masculinity.

Kashmir situation has jeopardised education of women. The same happened in the ULFA affected areas in Assam and LTTE-prone areas in Jaffna (Sri Lanka). The Christian fundamentalists in Latin America are no different. All of them use young women in suicide squads and as cannon fodder for their barbaric agenda. In the camps of Vishwa Hindu Parishad, young girls are brain-washed first with an ideological investment of communal education ("Muslims will outnumber Hindus", "Muslim men are lustful and Muslim women are breeders", "Muslims are born criminals", "Caste system is crucial for racial purity", "*Shudras* and *Ati-Shudras* are pollutants") and at the same time given training to use weapons (lathis, swords and daggers) (Vaz, 2003).

Communal mindset created by Hindutva forces is so powerful that young college students of the enlightened Wilson College got a humorous article based on stereotypes about "MUSLIM" as a murderer, drug seller, a cheater in cricket, kidnapper, terrorist, published. Its title is PAKISTANI MATH QUESTION PAPER. The very first question signifies man-woman relationship among the Muslims. It goes like this: "Abdul was sent to jail for murder. He has seven wives in his house. Abdul distributed money to his wives in such a proportion that the youngest and the most recent wife receives maximum and oldest wife gets minimum, and each wife gets double of her former competitor. Abdul has 1,700 rupees left in his house. Abdul's oldest wife needs at least 25 rupees per month. Find out the time when Abdul will have to break jail to come out (and come out sop) that his wives don't have to starve." There are innumerable websites with similar constructions that demonise Muslim men.

The most widely circulated cassettes of the speeches and slogans by Sadhvi Ritambhara, the crudest version of Hindutva ideology, provide Ram-centred and RSS-led perspective that has nothing in store for women but "agni pariksha" (i.e., enter the fire to prove chastity and purity). Sadhvi's speeches and pet slogan, "If there has to be bloodshed, let it happen once and for all" during Ram Janmabhoomi campaigns organized by Hindutva forces between 1986–1990 played crucial role in massacre of Muslims in the 1992 riots (Sarkar, 2001).

Ban on inter-caste, inter-religious and inter-racial marriages: Obsession about racial, caste and religious purity are so deep in the psyche of fundamentalists that have strong aversion against inter-mixing and inter-marriages among citizens of different caste groups, religious communities and racial backgrounds. Newspapers are full of incidences of torture, abduction, forced abortion, lynching, murder of newly married couples with different caste, religious, ethnic or racial backgrounds. Even the state and criminal justice system miserably fails to provide adequate protection to such marriages. Such couples have to face not only social boycott, but they also cannot get jobs, accommodation and school admissions for their children easily.

Conversion of husband or wife as a conditionality for "allowing" couples to get married is a logical extension of inward looking mentality generated by the fundamentalist mindset.

Communalized Violence Against Women

The communalized violence that women have experienced recently in Gujarat is unprecedented in terms of the degree of state complicity, the unashamed valourization of these acts of depravity, the horrific participation of women in the violence and the creation of an implacable wall of hatred that provides the reason and then the justification for its spiral effect. It took us fifty years to document excesses against women during the partition. One wonders how much longer it will take now.

The following poem by Lara Jesani vividly captures the pain and pathos of women victims of fundamentalist wrath and communal carnage whether they were women victims in 1992–93 Mumbai riots or women in refugee camps of Gujarat ten years later, in 2002–03:

> Eyes raining, without mere control,
> Scruples hurt, thus dew drops roll.
> Lightened, piercing, still with grief,
> Forever, staring in disbelief.
>
> Hearts melting, defences down,
> Afflicted feelings, all around.
> Timeless moments, of unending sorrow,
> Darkened scars, that none can borrow.
>
> Deep in hurdles, full with distress,
> Pleasures replaced, by pure sadness.
> Love's demise, of responsive pain,
> A day's repose, then it starts again.

In response to rising communal violence, several women's organizations in Mumbai have formed a united front to coordinate work regarding relief and rehabilitation based on the reports of fact-finding committees of riot affected areas in the rural, urban and tribal regions of Gujarat. Women's organizations such as Aawaaz-e-Niswan, Akshara, All India Democratic Women's Association, Documentation, Research and Training Centre of Justice and Peace Commission, Forum Against Oppression of Women, Forum for Women's Health, Maharashtra Mahila Parishad, Maharashtra Stree Abhyas Vyaspeeth, Mahila Daxata Samiti, Majlis, NFIW, Sakhya, Special Cell for Women and Children, Stree Manch, Stree Mukti Sangathana, Stree Sangam, Swadhar, Vacha, Women's Centre and Young Women Christian Association joined the commemoration of national protest day on 13 May 2002 against sexual assault, beating, rape and burning of women and young girls, the cutting open of a pregnant woman and killing of her foetus and the burning of babies and children.

They condemned this violence and demanded that FIRs should be registered, especially in all reported cases of sexual assault and violence against women, accepting testimonies of survivors as witnesses, in all police stations with copies made available to public groups. Because of the state and central governments' complicity, the women's groups felt the necessity of organizing a special public hearing on Gujarat carnage in front of an independent Women's Human Rights Commission (Nainar and Uma, 2003).

Areas of ethnic tension and caste/communal riots need special intervention in terms of workshops to unlearn chauvinistic values through role play, role reversal, psychotherapy and group counselling. Refugee camps of the victims of riots should provide security and development inputs for women and children. Gujarat riots have proved the devastating influence of high-tech 21st century VAW instigated by the fundamentalist and communal forces.

Violence and Health Issues of Women over the Life Cycle

As unborn children, women also face covert violence in terms of sex selection and overt violence in terms of female foeticide after the use of amniocentesis, chorion villai biopsy, sonography, ultrasound and imaging techniques.[1] IVF (In Vitro Fertilization) clinics (for assisted reproduction) are approached by infertile couples to produce sons. Doctors are advertising aggressively: "Invest Rs 500 now, save Rs 50,000 later", i.e., "If you get rid of your daughter now, you will not have to spend money on dowry".

As girls under five years of age, women in India face neglect in terms of medical care and education, sexual abuse and physical violence. As adolescent and adult women in the reproductive age group, they face early marriage, early pregnancy, sexual violence, domestic violence, dowry harassment, torture in case of infertility and if they fail to produce son, then face desertion/witch-hunt. The end-result is a high maternal mortality. Causes of maternal deaths in our country are haemorrhage, abortion, infection, obstructed labour, eclampsia (blood pressure during pregnancy), sepsis and anaemia. Proliferation of new reproductive technologies should be analysed in this context.

Sexual Violence and Mental Health

Sexual assault, molestation, rape, sexual harassment at workplace, child sexual abuse and nuisance calls cause psychological disturbances among girls and women. The trauma of sexual violence sparks off tension and anxiety at a dangerous level. Their mental health problems are manifested in anxiety, fear, avoidance, guilt, loss of efficiency, lack of coordination, depression, sexual dysfunction, substance abuse, relieving the traumatic incidents through memory, suicidal attempts, eating disorders, disturbed sleep patterns, fear of encountering such situation time and again, and the like. It is found that "women who undergo extreme sexual violence experience a loss of self and self-esteem following the shock inflicted on them. When there is a continuous period of traumatic stress, it becomes chronic, lessening the individual's ability to do any kind of constructive work" (Nair and Nair, 2002). Hence, this forms of male violence towards women is an important issue that demands public attention. Women's organizations have taken up this issue at local, national and global levels.

The United Nations and VAW

As per Convention on Elimination of All Forms of Discrimination Against Women (CEDAW), "All states are obliged to prevent and eliminate all forms of violence against women and girls". Beijing Declaration, Platform for Action, and the UN World Conference on Women, China, 1995 gave a mandate to all member countries of the UN to devise action plan against VOW. Most of the countries in the region have ratified CEDAW. Some have however refused. Indonesia has even refused to ratify the declarations of three major UN Conferences that discussed VAW: The Vienna Declaration, (1993) the Declaration of Elimination of VAW (1994) and the CEDAW (1995).

World Social Forum and VAW: Global concern against VAW is witnessed in the number of workshops, conferences and women's courts during World Social Forums.

Laws concerning VAW

India was the first nation to enact the Family Courts Act (1984). Domestic Violence Bill (2002) has been passed by Indian Parliament as Domestic Violence Act, 2005. Women's movement has pushed for legislation to provide protection for abused women. After 10 years of lobbying, Malaysia became the first country to enact Domestic Violence Act, 1994. It has been studied by Islamic countries. In a strong state of Singapore, under reporting of VAW is a major problem.

There is a need for broadening the definition of domestic violence to include violence against women, senior citizens (abuse of "mentally unfit" certificate), incest and rape by family members and relatives forcing women and girls into prostitution (International Commission of Jurist, 1995).

Under the Indian Penal Code (IPC), the following sections are applied in cases of VAW:

Section	*Nature of Offence*
304B	Dowry death/murder
354	Criminal assault of women to outrage women's modesty
366	Kidnap, abduction and marriage of a women by force.
366A	Procurement of a minor girl
366B	Import of girl from a foreign country
374	Rape
376A	Intercourse by a man with his wife during judicial separation
376B	Intercourse by a public servant with woman in his custody
376C	Intercourse by superintendent of jail, remand home with woman in his custody
376D	Intercourse by any member of the management or staff of a hospital with any woman in that hospital
498A	Husband or in-laws subjecting a woman to cruelty
509	Word, gesture or act intended to insult the modesty of a woman

Legal awareness about VAW is extremely important. We must know that in India, the following legal provisions are made to tackle VAW:

- Dowry Prohibition Act, 1961.
- Indecent Representation of Women (Prohibition) Act, 1986 to take action against sexist portrayal of women in the audio-visual print and electronic media, pornography and cyber-porn.
- Prevention of Immoral Traffic (in women and children) Act, 1987 to crack down on prostitution.
- Commission on Sati Prevention Act, 1987 to fight widow burning and its glorification.
- Supreme Court Directive against Sexual Harassment at Workplace, 1997.
- The Pre-Natal Diagnostic Techniques (Regulation and Prevention of Misuse) Amendment Act, 2002 to stop sex selection at pre-conception stage as well as of an unborn foetus.

Country-specific campaigns for legal reforms by human/women rights organizations such as Pre-Natal Diagnostic Technique Act (India), Hudood Ordinance (Pakistan) and family laws and customary practices need global solidarity. Public interest litigations to deal with sexual harassment at workplace should be filed by the NGOs. Women in India need a comprehensive Women's Protection Act that can take care of both civil and criminal matters because even if women fight in civil courts for their rights concerning marriage, divorce, custody of children, alimony, maintenance, property, access to matrimonial or ancestral home, they have to face violence from their near and dear ones. We need common legislation for the region to deal with cross-country trafficking of women and girls for sex trade and organ transplant.

Police station: VAW is a cognizable offence against the state. If you face VAW or see it happening in the neighbourhood, public place or at a workplace, you can immediately contact police demanding inquiry and get the FIR filed. You should make three copies – one for the victim, one should be submitted to the police station and do not forget to take an official stamp and signature of the police officer in-charge on the third copy. These documentary proofs are extremely important in the court of law.

Court proceedings: Provide moral support to the victim and brief her to provide accurate details in chronological order about violence. She must stick to the same version; changing position during cross-examination may go against her.

Many cases of VAW also get resolved in the neighbourhood committee, community organizations and *lok adalats* (People's Courts). We must remember that VAW is a manifestation of unequal power relations between men and women. If women are empowered by the community and official support, we can tilt the balance in favour of "VAW-free society".

Media and VAW

Action programme for media to prevent VAW should be as follows:

- Monitoring of covert and overt VAW in print and audio-visual media and encouragement for public debate for mass education on construction of man-woman relationship, sex stereotypes, glorification of angry, aggressive HE-man and masochist woman.
- Media alternatives for non-violent relationship between men and women. "Suffering in silence is not a virtue", can be an appeal of male protagonists.
- Demand for portrayal of women's agency as an active contributor for social/human development.
- Positive projection of female headed households and special problems faced by such households jobs, housing, schooling of their children, property right, etc.

Self-defence and Assertiveness Training

Ideal solution for prevention of VAW is a multi-pronged approach involving female autonomy, economic empowerment and improved status of girl child. Counselling for personality development and assertiveness training should teach women various techniques of handling acts of violence and aggressive behaviour, e.g., use of loud voice to prevent violence, need for physical power to handle violence, etc. Self-defence courses – karate and country-specific martial arts – should be made available for women and girls. Dealing with anorexia nervosa and bulimia-eating disorders due to violence or anticipation of violence should be treated as an important issue and included in the module on self-defence training programmes.

State and Civil Society Initiatives

The National Policy for Empowerment of Women, 2001 of Government of India declares: "All forms of violence against women, physical and mental, whether at domestic or societal levels, including those arising from customs, traditions or accepted practices, shall be dealt with effectively with a view to eliminate its incidence. Institutions and mechanisms/schemes for assistance will be created and strengthened for prevention of such violence, including sexual harassment at workplace and customs like dowry. For rehabilitation of the victims of violence and for taking effective action against perpetrators of such violence, a special emphasis will also be laid on programmes and measures to deal with trafficking in women and girls".

"Because Personal is Political" – a document published by Tata Institute of Social Sciences, Mumbai – provides valuable insight into collaborative venture between social workers and the Mumbai Police during 1984–1994. Documentation of 10 years of work against VAW also provides important understanding about legal provisions for redressal of domestic disputes through establishment of Family Court (as per the Family Court Act, 1984). Women's Cell in the Police Commissioner's office was established in 1984. Civil matters were handled by professional social workers appointed by TISS and police intervened to deal with criminal matters that included domestic violence, sexual violence, physical and psychological cruelty and murder.

According to Philippines National Police, in 1994, every 6 hours, one woman was raped. In the same way, 40 per cent of women in Malaysia are victims of physical abuse. This scary statistics highlights the need for a women's cell in the police stations in Asian and Pacific countries.

Two prominent items in the agenda for action to combat VAW are:

- Training for the police force, judiciary, doctors and hospital staff, lawyers, media, politicians, administrators and the members of Women's Commissions.
- Resource kit for workers in caring professions that teaches various techniques of handling acts of violent and aggressive behaviour.

Empowering women through of feminist counselling (Baaco-Pascual, 2001) is a result of 4-pronged approach and was implemented by the Arugaan Ng Kalakasan in Philippines:

1. Creative strategies for mobilization of resources against VAW in terms of consciousness raising and action.
2. Telephone counselling as a feminist alternative for abused women in intimate relationship.
3. FACTS against MYTHS exercise for public education on VAW.
4. Defining policewomen's role for empowerment of women victims of violence.

Practical Ways of Tackling the Issue of VAW

If we firmly believe that women's rights are human rights, we have to devise practical ways of tackling the issue of VAW. We have to be proactive to stop violence by direct intervention and prevent violence through public education of the civil society and affirmative action by the criminal justice system.

As individuals we must understand that to perpetrate violence or to be a mute witness to violence, both are same. Hence, we should combat VAW in personal life through prompt action and in public life through demonstrations, rallies, sit-ins, and writing and speaking against it from public platforms. To counter myths about VAW that lead to victim blaming ("Women ask for it", "Women provoke it", "Women enjoy it as sado-masochist relationship with her tormentor") is extremely important to legitimize women's experience of VAW and penalize the tormentor. Women victims of VAW should be encouraged to speak out and not suffer in silence. Tormentors' misdeeds should be publicized in the neighbourhood so that the victim gets timely support in case of physical and psychological violence. Phone numbers of the nearest police station and one-stop crisis centres in the nearest government or municipal hospital should be found out from the telephone directory or "Help Line" column of daily newspapers.

Training workshops for self-defence techniques and assertiveness among women should be organized because physical fitness is as important as self-confidence, presence of mind and voice training (lung power and tongue power) to disarm the tormentor.

Public education can be imparted through exhibitions, film screening followed by discussion, poster campaigns, slide shows, power point presentations, street plays, songs and ballets, and role reversal techniques on the theme of VAW. Sometimes, creative expressions are more powerful than dead statistics or lecture.

Conclusion

Women's organizations in the last two decades have brought the issue of growing VAW on the public agenda. We have also realized that encouraging men's involvement as partners for just and humane society to create VAW-free life is extremely important. Research has shown that violence is learned, not innate behaviour. Sensitizing of men and boys on gender stereotypes as well as the concept of masculinity that subordinates women, should be done by educational institutions, media and citizens groups such as YMCA. Helping men to challenge and unlearn those norms that condone violence is an uphill task. Setting up complementary rehabilitative programmes for abusers needs an interdisciplinary approach and collaboration of state, civil society and human rights groups. Majority of social workers in Asia recommend a balance of punitive and rehabilitative measures to change violent behaviour of men (Satia and Hoi, 2001).

We should invite creative expressions on VAW from children and discuss them to make the next generation gender-sensitive and free from internalization of violent behaviour with girls and women. Sensitive use of communication media, proactive role of the state, decriminalization of politics, public education in the community and workplace as well as an active intervention of civil society can prevent VAW in our society. It is important to promote multicultural ethos, secular humanism, respect for diversity and peaceful resolution of conflicting opinions to stop societal violence in general and VAW in particular.

Note

1. Patel, Vibhuti (1992) "Girl Child: An Endangered Species?" in Viney Kripal (ed.), *The Girl Child in 20th Century Indian Literature*, Sterling Publications Pvt. Ltd., New Delhi, p. 9.

References

Abdullah, R. 2001. 'Indicators of Women's Mental Health and Well-being' *Arrows for Change,* Vol. 7, No. 3, Kuala Lumpur, Malaysia, p.12. www.arrow.org.my

Baaco-Pascula, S. 2001. 'Empowering Women Through Feminist Counselling in the Philippines', *ARROW for Change,* Vol. 7, No. 3, Kuala Lumpur, Malaysia, p. 4. www.arrow.org.my

Chang, J. 2002. 'Online Sexual Violence and Policies', *Asian Women*, Research Institute of Asian Women, Sookmyung Women's University, Korea.

Chee, H.L. 2002. 'Genomics and Health: Ethical, Legal and Social Implications for Developing Countries', *Issues in Medical Ethics*, January–March, p. 148. medicalethics.India.org

Dewan, Ritu. 2002. 'What Does Azadi Mean to You'. *In* Urvashi Butalia (ed.) *Speaking Peace: Women's Voices from Kashmir.* Delhi: Kali for Women.

Engineer, Asghar Ali (ed.). 2003. *The Gujarat Carnage,* Delhi: Orient Longman.

Fernandes, G and Ray, C.S. 2002. 'Raids, Rescue', Rehabilitation, Research Unit, College of Social Work, Nirmala Niketan, Mumbai.

Ganatara, B., Hirve, S. and Rao V. N. 2001. 'Sex Selective Abortion: Evidence From a Community-based Study in Western India', *Asia Pacific Population Journal*, UN ESCAP, Economic and Social Commission for Asia and the Pacific, Bangkok, Thailand, Vol. 16, No. 2, June.

Herring, S.C. 'Cyber Violence and Gender: Suggestions Through Analysis of Cases', *Asian Women*, Research Institute of Asian Women, Sookmyung Women's University, Korea, pp. 187–212.

Hitchcock, Jayne. 2002. 'The Wild Wild Web: Cyber Stalking', *Asian Women*, Research Institute of Asian Women, Sookmyung Women's University, Korea, pp.175–155.

International Commission of Jurists (1995) Women and the Law in the Pacific, Geneva.

Jesani, A. 2002. 'Violence Against Women: Health and Health Care Issues: A Review of Selected Indian Works', *Samyukta: A Journal of Women's Studies*, Vol. II, No. 2, July, p. 57. Website: www.samyukta,org.

Karkal, M. 1991. 'Abortion Laws and the Abortion Situation in India', *Issues in Reproductive and Genetic Engineering*, Vol. 4, No. 3, pp. 223–30.

Kramarae, C. and Spender, D. (eds.). 2000. *International Encyclopedia of Women: Global Women's Issues and Knowledge*, New York and London: Routledge, pp. 2014–15.

Nainar, Vahida and Saumya Uma. 2003. *Combatting impunity: A Compilation of Articles on the International Criminal Court and Its Relevance in India*. Women's Research and Action Network, Mumbai.

Lawyers Collective. 2000. Positive Dialogue, HIV/AIDS Unit, Mumbai, Newsletter 6, August, p. 4.

Lee, K.H. 2002. 'Cyber Violence and Gender', *Asian Women*, Research Institute of Asian Women, Sookmyung Women's University, Korea, pp. 217–233.

Manchanda, Rita (ed.). 2001. *Women, War and Peace in South Asia: Beyond Victimhood to Agency*. Delhi: Sage Publications.

Nair, J. and Nair H. 2002. 'Gendering Health', *Samyukta,* Vol. 2, No. 1, January, p. 44.

Nainar, Vahida and Saumya Uma. 2003. *Combatting Impunity: A Compilation of Articles on the International Criminal Court and Its Revelance in India,* Women's Research and Action Network, Mumbai

Patel, Vibhuti. 2002. *Women's Challenges of the New Millennium*. Delhi. Gyan Publishing House. pp. 116–127.

—. 2003. 'Sons are Rising, Daughters are Setting', *Humanscape*, Vol, 10, No. IX, September. Also on the web: www.humanscapeindia.net.

—. 'Women's Right to Mental Health', *Vikalpa*, Vikas Adhyayan Kendra, Mumbai, Vol. X, No. 3, pp. 5–18. Also published in the Web Journal–*India Together,* January, 2004.

—. 2004. 'Globalisation and Declining Sex Ratio', Workshop at World Social Forum, January 18, 2004. Also published in the web journal *The Quarterly Journal of Opinion,* http://wwwthequarterly.net, July, 2003.

Pevrin, Jean-Pierre. 1997. *Afghanistan Goes to Absurd Lengths to Implement Islamic Laws.* Women Living Under Muslim Law. Dossier 17. Paris. June, pp. 106–110.

Poonanchit-Korsieporn, A. 2002. 'Research Notes on Violence Against Women in Thailand', *Asian Women*. Thailand: Chulalongkorn University. pp. 81–93.

Sarkar, Tanika. 2001. *Hindu Wife, Hindu Nation-Community, Religion and Cultural Nationalism.* New Delhi: Permanent Black.

Satia, J. and M. Hoi. 2001. *Innovations,* Special Number on Violence Against Women. Malaysia: Selangore. Vol. 9, p. 120.

Sen, A.K. 1992. 'Missing Women', *British Medical Journal,* No. 304, March.

Shin, Y.H. 2002. 'Cyber Sexual Violence and Ethics for Regulation', *Asian Women*, Research Institute of Asian Women, Sookmyung Women's University, Korea, pp. 147–173.

Shrestha, A.K., Tamang, Meera and Sharma, Kabita. 2002. 'Determinants of Induced Abortion and Subsequent Reproductive Behaviour Among Women in Three Urban Districts of Nepal' *In* Mundigo, A. and Indriso, C. (eds.) *Abortion in Developing World*. New Delhi: Vistaar Publications. p. 167.

Shyam, K. 2002. 'Smut Parties in a New Pack', *Indian Express, Mumbai Newsline,* November 3.

Vaz, Hubert. 2003. 'The VHP Back in Training'. *Indian Express Newsline*. 19th May.

WHO. 1996. World Health Organisation, Geneva.

4

Sexual Harassment at Workplace

RENUKA MUKADAM AND PRACHI PATWARDHAN

Sexual harassment at workplace is an issue that has slowly been coming out of the closet. In a society where the mere mention of the word 'sex' or 'sexuality' is a taboo, this is no mean achievement. In a patriarchal society, women's sexuality and their reproductive power has been controlled by men and used as a means of subjugating them to their wishes. We have seen time and again that men use sexuality of women to make other men feel ashamed, who are their husbands or fathers. Raping wives/sisters is often used as a means to "get even" with the male opponents. Thus sex is used as a power play, and its abuse cuts across the rural, urban caste, class, religious and regional divisions in our diverse country.

The understanding of sexual harassment as an issue necessitates an analysis of people's perception of gender roles. Gender role stereotypes dictate that women should be at home, caring for the children and doing other domestic chores, and it is the man who has to go out and earn money to feed the family. As a result, society finds it difficult to accept women in the workplace, more so in traditionally male-dominated professions like engineering, aviation, mechanics, carpentry, bus/rickshaw/train/taxi driving etc. Patriarchy looks upon women's employment outside as a threat to the male domination and supremacy.

With education opportunities opening up for women, many more women are entering the organized workforce at a fast pace. The problem of sexual harassment has been surfacing more as recognition and acceptance of their contribution is relatively slower. Globalization may have created jobs for women but most of these are low level and dead-end jobs, creating more insecurity. It has led to a 'feminization' of jobs whereby only certain jobs are available for women, and they have to do either those, or then restrict themselves to housework. With the emphasis on labour and time saving technology in the market, women are more likely to be retrenched than men. Thus, the 'labour saving' technology ends up becoming 'women replacing' technology. Besides, working outside the home does not give women respite from the domestic responsibilities; hence, they often have to play superwomen in order to be able to balance both. All this creates immense job insecurity, especially so for women, as everyone knows that they are the "last to be hired and the first to be fired". This background is essential to understand the context within witch sexual harassment takes place, and it also helps understand the difficulty women face talking about the problem openly.

The Supreme Court of India, for the first time, acknowledged the existence of sexual harassment at workplace, and the need for legal recourse for the same. In response to a petition filed by women's groups, the apex court passed a landmark judgment on the issue of sexual harassment at workplace on 13 August 1997. Recognizing sexual harassment as a human rights violation, the judgment, called the Vishaka judgment, defines sexual harassment, and assigns responsibility of prevention and redress of complaints to the employer. The judgment also keeps up to India's obligations under CEDAW, which it has ratified in 1979.

It was in the year 1995 that Bhanwari Devi, a Saathin – a village development worker – was gangraped in a Rajasthan village by five upper caste men of the village, as a 'punishment' for campaigning against child marriage and subsequently putting a stop to one such marriage in the upper caste family. Bhanwari Devi faced a lot of problems when she decided to fight back, right from hostile police to biased and patriarchal judiciary and an unfavourable judgment in the Sessions Court stating that it is not possible for five upper caste men of a village to rape a dalit woman. A number of women's rights groups across the country came together over this, and filed a petition in the Supreme Court of India saying that this was a matter of sexual harassment at workplace and that the court should give certain directions in this matter. It was as a result of this struggle that the Vishaka judgment came about.

The Vishaka Judgment

Sexual harassment includes such unwelcome sexually determined behaviour (whether directly or by implication) as:

(a) physical contact and advances;
(b) a demand or request for sexual favours;
(c) sexually coloured remarks;
(d) showing pornography; and
(e) any other unwelcome physical, verbal or non-verbal conduct of sexual nature.

The judgment mandates that the rules/regulations of government and public sector bodies relating to conduct and discipline should include rules/regulations prohibiting sexual harassment and provide for appropriate penalties in such rules against the offender. In government sectors it mandates the necessary changes in the service and conduct rules. As regards private employers steps should be taken to include the aforesaid prohibitions in the standing orders under the Industrial Employment (Standing Orders) Act, 1940.

The judgment also says that every workplace should have a Complaints Committee (CC) to look into the prevention of sexual harassment and resolution of complaints. The CC should be headed by a woman and at least half of its members should be women. Further, to prevent the possibility of any undue pressure or influence from senior levels, such committee should involve a third party, either NGO or other body or an individual, who is familiar with the issue of sexual harassment. The CC should investigate the complaints in a confidential and time-bound manner. It also ask the government department concerned to report it annually on the complaints and action taken by them.

The onus and the responsibility to provide for harassment-free and a safe working environment at the workplace has been put on the employers, thus ensuring it is not 'personal problem' between the aggrieved and the alleged harasser. Thus, the management and the employers are to make sure that a CC is put in place and in compliance with the guidelines performs its functions of a preventive and a proactive body as far as the issue of sexual harassment is concerned.

The 'third party' form of harassment has also been given recognition as per the guidelines, that is, harassment by an 'insider' to the service provider, and or vice versa.

Understanding sexual harassment at workplace, as a phenomenon, and the popular perception about it, in the background of a patriarchal society:

The one important consideration is that it is hardly recognized as an issue. There seems to be a general tendency to trivialize the issue, belittle it or ignore it. One of the possible reasons for this could be the failure to understand that a workplace is an extension of the patriarchal society of which it is a part, and hence the same power structures operate there as they do elsewhere. Another important issue to consider is the gradual entry of women in the various fields of work, especially the formal sector, many of which have traditionally been male-dominated. Sometimes their entry in government jobs has been through reservation in appointments and in professional education. It is important to understand the effect this would have on the men and how they may take this as a sudden 'invasion' of their 'space'.

The first query raised is why should women work? Isn't their zone of confinement the home and the hearth? It is widely felt that women should not come to the places that they are not welcome in, and then complain of harassment. There is an understanding that women have to become "one of the boys" in order to work in an office. As women are given extra and unnecessary rights that are often denied to men, why have then reservation for women at various levels? It is a complete farce that on the one hand you talk of equality of men and women, and demand for special privileges and a separate set of rights and reservations for women, on the other. This especially is a major complaint expressed by professional students (males) as there is 30 per cent reservation in professional courses for women, and the boys feel that the girls waste a seat as they get married and do not work.

Another common misunderstanding is that women employees are unproductive, and are not sincere about their work, hence they are targeted. Or, it is also felt that because they do not do their work and are pulled up for the same, they make false and malicious complaints of sexual harassment at workplace. The women have to put in twice the efforts to be considered successful or efficient.

Myths and stereotypes on the issue and the traps that these create are largely drawn from the above mentioned view. Some of the most common ones are as follows:

Myth: Women who say 'No' actually mean 'Yes'. Saying 'No' is their style and actually they mean 'Yes'.

Fact: A common myth used by men to justify sexual aggression. This also nullifies all the protests made by the woman, and puts the blame on her.

Myth: Women enjoy eve teasing/sexual harassment.

Fact: Women find eve teasing/sexual harassment a humiliating, painful and frightening experience.

Myth: The seriousness of sexual harassment is exaggerated.

Fact: Sexual harassment can be devastating. Studies indicate that most harassment has nothing to do with flirtation, sincere sexual or social interest. Rather, it is offensive, often frightening and insulting to women. It can have serious and far-reaching consequences for both the victim and the organization. It is due to this that women are hesitant to report abut their experiences and hence sexual harassment goes unnoticed.

Myth: Eve teasing is harmless flirtation. Women who object have no sense of humour.

Fact: Behaviour that is unwelcome cannot be considered harmless, or funny. Sexual harassment is defined by its impact on the woman, rather than the intent of the perpetrator.

Myth: Only women who are provocatively dressed are sexually harassed. Decent women do not get sexually harassed. There is also a strong belief that each woman has to define her own limits and if she is being over-friendly with men, she is inviting trouble.

Fact: This is a classic way of shifting the blame from the harasser to the woman. This blaming of the woman is not only wrong; it is one of the most powerful instruments used to control women in our society. It serves to encourage the harasser. Women have a right to act, dress and move around freely without the threat of harassment or violence.

Myth: Many women make up and report false stories of sexual harassment to get back at their employers or others who have angered them.

Fact: Research shows that less than 1 per cent of the complaints are false. In fact, women rarely file complaints even when they are justified in doing so. Sexual harassment is a largely under-reported phenomenon. Women know that they are going to be subject to gossip and character assassination, hence, they are hesitant to complain, making false complaints becomes a very far-fetched possibility given all this.

Myth: Sexual harassment is not a common phenomenon.

Fact: In a study conducted by Saakshi, a Delhi-based NGO, at five different centres in India, 72 per cent of the women respondents had heard or encountered cases of sexual harassment at the workplace. The same study showed that 42 per cent women said that women generally experience sexually inappropriate behaviour at the workplace.

Myth: A happily married, middle-aged, respectable, educated, high-profile job man who has children, especially daughters, will not indulge in sexual harassment.

Fact: Statistics and cases of sexual harassment do not show any particular profile of a person who has indulged in sexual harassment. It is important to remember that sexual harassment is not as much about sex as it is about power.

Any person in a position of power can harass a person over whom he can utilize that power.

Why Prevention?

One generally finds an apathetic attitude when it comes to prevention on this issue, the general tendency is, let something happen, then we can deal with it. Why work towards prevention when this may never happen?

- Because it is unprofessional and illegal.
- Because sexual harassment is a form of discriminatory behaviour, which carries with it an implied threat to the woman's employment.
- Because employees have a right to work in an environment that is free from sexual harassment and employers are responsible for providing this to all workers.
- Because it also has the following effects on employers:
  - (a) Lower productivity and employee morale.
  - (b) Other employees lose faith in your ability to lead, manage and stop unwanted behaviour.
  - (c) Increased costs for hiring and training of new employees.
  - (d) High legal costs and a poor public image.
- Because sexual harassment has lasting emotional, psychological and physical effects on the women who face it. Some of these are as follows:
  - (a) Psychological and emotional effects like revulsion, anger, disgust, shame, guilt, confusion, anxiety, nervousness, depression and low self-esteem.
  - (b) Physical effects like sleeplessness, headache, nausea, high blood pressure and ulcers.
  - (c) Financial/work-related effects like job losses, financial losses, low concentration on work, which could lead to accidents etc. and in turn affect the work.

Some Important Studies

Many scholars and organizations working for the cause of women's rights conducted studies on sexual harassment at workplace. In this section, we present the findings of some important studies. To start with, a study conducted by Saakshi, in five states with a group of 2,400 men and women from a cross-section of workplaces and hierarchies, reveals that:

- 80 per cent of respondents say sexual harassment exists at their workplace.
- 49 per cent have encountered cases of sexual harassment.
- 41 per cent have experienced or known women who have faced unwanted sexual behaviour at work.
- 53 per cent say men and women do not have equal opportunities at work. The same numbers of persons say women are treated unfairly by their supervisor/employer/co-worker/fellow student.
- 58 per cent have never heard of the Vishaka guidelines.
- Only 20 per cent respondents say their organizations have implemented the guidelines.

Similarly, another survey on sexual harassment at workplace, conducted by Sanhita, in Kolkata, in early 2000, among 525 men and women belonging to the government sector (like police, railways, tax, etc.), public sector (like banks, airlines, etc.) and private sector (like advertising, hotels etc.), show that 35 per cent women had experienced sexual harassment at their workplaces. When asked about the fear of sexual harassment, 52 per cent women, while denying having faced any sexual harassment, expressed the apprehension that they can face it in the future. The survey also indicates that the perpetrators of sexual harassment could be the boss/employer, colleague, subordinate, client/outsider, or just anybody from any level. When asked as to why women do not complain, most, i.e., 83 per cent, respondents indicated social stigma as the reason for not complaining, followed by fear of reprisal by 41 per cent. Yet in another study conducted by India Centre for Human Rights and Law and the Research Centre for Women's Studies (SNDT University), under the aegis of the Maharashtra State Commission for Women, in the J.J. Hospital and the Grant Medical College of Mumbai, 12.39 per cent of the respondents reported being harassed on the campus of the hospital/college, and 26.90 per cent of the respondents reported knowing other women who were harassed on the campus. The study thus showed that overall the students were more vulnerable to harassment. When asked whether they were likely to face harassment in the future too, 25.21 per cent of the respondents replied in the affirmative.

More or less similar findings were reported in a study conducted by India Centre for Human Rights and Law, in collaboration with the Sociology Department of the Sophia College. The study covered a small sample of 76 women, of which 51% belonged to the private sector, 25 per cent to the government sector and 17 per cent were self-employed or professionals. When asked about the understanding of harassment, 61 per cent of the respondents identified physical misbehaviour as sexual harassment. Regarding the prevalence of sexual harassment, 25 per cent said that it occurs frequently, 36 per cent rarely, and according to only 7 per cent sexual harassment does not occur at all. Of the total respondents, 53 per cent said that they had either witnessed or had the knowledge of sexual harassment of someone else. Of these women, 42 per cent said that their friend was harassed, 33 per cent said they knew a colleague/junior/senior at workplace who was harassed, 8 per cent said that they knew of an acquaintance and an equal number knew a relative who was harassed. Even 46 per cent of the total women have experienced sexual harassment at workplace, of which 43 per cent women said that had occurred in their present place of work. Likewise, 31 per cent of women who experienced sexual harassment said that they faced verbal harassment such as slang remarks, talking on sexual intercourse, comments on dress and figure, asked to sit closer, etc., 29 per cent faced unwanted physical contacts, followed by 20 per cent having faced demands for sexual favour such as invitation to join at a pub, lunch or dinner, pressurizing to please clients, condition of increasing the pay if they went out with the boss, etc., 11 per cent said that they faced non-verbal harassment such as staring, and an equal number said that they faced emotional harassment such as being given odd working hours, and creating an uncomfortable environment. A Similar percentage of women have, however, found it difficult to share the nature of sexual harassment they experienced. Some women tried more than one coping mechanism in dealing with sexual harassment and therefore the percentage indicated in this section are based on the multiple responses to the question, what women did about the harassment. One significant response made by 42 per cent women was that they chose to ignore the harassment whereas 31 per cent said that they tried to avoid the harasser. Similarly, 42 per cent said they confronted the harasser, 25 per cent said they complained to the authority, and 22 per cent said they chose to confide in a colleague. A significant number (23%) left the job and very few (9%) approached unions. When asked about whether they knew the Supreme Court guidelines, only 24 per cent of the respondents answered in the affirmative, while an overwhelming 64% said that they did not know about the guidelines. Colleagues have displayed both support and lack of support to the harassed person, which many times lead to women feeling further helpless and traumatized. Support from colleague is bound to strengthen the woman and can help in reducing the trauma of lone battle of fighting sexual harassment. It is evident that women feel comfortable with their colleagues or close friends to talk about harassment but are not very comfortable about approaching seniors or authorities. The relationship of trust and confidence that a woman will be heard and believed, lies more with the colleagues than any other personnel at workplace. This although does not guarantee action, definitely ensures support much needed by the harassed person.

Implementation of the Judgment

After more than a decade's time of the passing of Vishaka judgment by the Supreme Court of India, one sees that while some employers have taken steps to comply with the guidelines, most others have not. In most states, the steps taken have been very inadequate. For instance, the Chandigarh government has only circulated the guidelines to subordinate cells and units, and has left the Crime against Women Cell to handle complaints. There has been no amendment in the Civil Service Rules, or the Industrial Employees Standing Orders Act, nor have they established a committee. Rajasthan, which is the state from where the case, which led to the judgment, had come, has only distributed some pamphlets and amended the Civil Service Rules. There has been no committee, and no other steps have been taken. Some states like Delhi have however set up committees and also amended their service rules, but have been unable to make a dent in the private sector. The Industrial Employees (Standing Orders) Act has not been amended in most states.

As far as Maharashtra is concerned, a committee has been set up and it abides by the guidelines; however, it is just one state-level committee, based in Mumbai, making it a very impractical mechanism and highly inaccessible to women from all over the state. The circulars state that the committee may be approached in the event of a complaint and the list of members on the committee is also enumerated. What it does not clarify is exactly how a woman who is working in a remote primary health centre somewhere in a rural area, is expected to make a complaint to a committee sitting to Mumbai, and follow-up on the case. Thus, even if the judgment has been implemented in letter, it has not been implemented in spirit, and so far we are not aware of any district-level government offices having any committees/cells to deal with the problem, nor are we aware of any directions given to them in this regard.

Some Central Government departments are oblivious to the very existence of such a judgment, all this despite government notifications to the effect of implementing Vishaka. Efforts have been largely ad-hoc, in response to cases, but not from the perspective of prevention. The possible reasons for this apathy towards the issue could be fear of further repercussions, concerns of negative image and of "putting things in the minds of people", lack of preventive outlook and also lack of knowledge about the adverse impact that sexual harassment can have on the productivity of the workers. Where the efforts to implement have been taken, there is a lack of endeavour to let the workers know about the same. So, although there may be a committee, and circulars may have been issued regarding the same, these circulars have been sent only to the departmental heads and it is left to their discretion to inform the employees about it. Efforts to put up the provisions and names of committee members in a place where employees can easily see them have not even been envisaged, with a very few exceptions.

However, there is the proverbial silver lining to every cloud. Due to the changes in the Civil Service Rules, some Municipal Corporations in Maharashtra and certain hospitals etc. coming under them, have taken the matter seriously, and are in the process of setting up mechanisms to that effect. The other progressive step has been from universities; due to certain research studies and press coverage of incidents, they have come up and have set up special cells to tackle the problem.

The private sector has been very slow in responding and very few have been pro-active in this matter. It has also been found that sometimes they have woken up to the issue after a specific incident, like the recent Infosys case. Some organizations, which are pro-active in their approach, have used their own creative ways to implement the judgment and also to make it effective, and to maintain a good working atmosphere.

Vishaka has benefited working women by giving them the right to a safe working environment and to an in-house complaints mechanism to enable quick redressal without going to the court. It proposes to provide a safe and gender-friendly atmosphere to men and women enabling them to work without any fears and antagonism. It has the potential to empower women about their rights, if efforts are made in that direction. The press has played a very important role in the generation of awareness and has helped the organizations by reporting cases and following them through, thus giving visibility to the issue, and reaching the information about the Vishaka guidelines out to working women and men.

All the efforts made so far, however, have been in the organized sector – be it in government offices or in private companies. The biggest challenge for groups working on sexual harassment remains with implementing the judgement in the unorganized sector where a vast majority of women workers are employed. Just as this large chunk of force in the country is denied the benefits of other labour laws, same is the case as far as this issue is concerned. Needless to say, given the lack of structure and job security in the unorganized sector, women working here are more vulnerable to harassment. Where the workers have some organized group/union, it has been instrumental in getting the woman justice, but again these victories have been few and far between.

A lot of ground is still to be covered. Trade unions in general continue to remain aloof from the issue in most places, as it puts one of their members against another. The level of awareness among women employers, trade unions and employers' fora remains dismal. Although there are groups working on the issue, the efforts are scattered and very local in orientation. Groups working on the issue, and other partners, need to come together for a sustained campaign on this issue, One such effort has been related to the Medha Kotwal case. The campaign emerged from a case in the M.S. University in Baroda, where despite a complaints committee, justice was not being done to the aggrieved woman. A letter written to the Supreme Court regarding this matter, by Medha Kotwal of Aalochana in Pune, was converted into a writ petition, and the apex court asked the states to file affidavits regarding the steps taken by them to implement the Vishaka judgment.

All this sparked off a national level campaign, and the groups jointly asked for certain provisions to strenghten Vishaka. In order to achieve this, there was a national level consultation among groups working on the issue, and a rejoinder has been filed in the Supreme Court asking for certan changes in the Vishaka judgment. The case is still being followed up in the Supreme Court of India, but as of now, the court has issued notices to several national level institutions representing various professions and work sectors, asking them to take steps to implement the guidelines. Some of these are Bar Council of India, Institute of Chartered Accountants, Medical Council of India, Press Council of India, Reserve Bank of India and Architects Council of India etc.

Looking Forward: Challenges in the Field

The most important challenge is to get employers understand that this is an issue needing preventive approach, and that they should not really be waiting for cases to come up before acting. By establishing a mechanism and adopting a policy, they will only be ensuring an open and friendly environment in their workplace and not really putting things in the minds of women. Also, to convince them that it is ridiculous to think that just because they have a mechanism in place, suddenly women all over the organization are going to leave their work and start making complaints of sexual harassment.

When the alleged harasser is a highly placed person, victimization of the complainant and the witnesses and supporters is very common, and can also be done in a subtle manner. This makes women feel that even if they complain, nothing is going to happen. Ignoring is the most common tactic used by women when dealing with sexual harassment. From experience we know that it is a long battle, hence, the challenge is to tell the women that they are in for struggle, and still to encourage them to fight and not ignore.

Women feel that when some women do keep friendly relations with the bosses, they get favours, and the others are discriminated against, hence, there should be a certain code of conduct for both men and women. It is also shared that sometimes an affair which has gone sour may lead to allegations of sexual harassment by the women, hence, workplaces should discourage affairs between their employees, especially where the man is in a position of power.

5
The Violence of Stigmatization

MEENA SARASWATHI SESHU

Working with women in prostitution and sex work for the past eight years in the HIV/AIDS prevention programme has helped us address our own double standards and bias while dealing with issues related to sexuality and prostitution.

As our involvement with the women we worked with deepened, our beliefs, ideas and notions about prostitution and women in prostitution underwent a sea change. Our perception of prostitution as "exploitation, victimization, oppression, loose, immoral, illegal", was shaken to the core.

Indeed, it was not merely our ideas and beliefs that had to be questioned and reformulated but even the very use of language to describe the women had to be transformed. 'Whore', 'harlot', 'veshya' – have been used as abuses for the 'fallen woman' – has been the subject of much public discourse. We have tried to help reclaim some of the terminology, and assert identities with positive meaning. We revised our vocabulary to weed out words that reinforce the stigmatization and marginalization of women in prostitution. Besides, we realized that the terminology used for generations by mainstream society to refer to the 'fallen woman' was more often than not derogatory, within the moral space of sacredness. The need to reclaim womanhood also became necessary since this sanctified moral space refused to acknowledge the fact that the very identity (of being a woman) was obliterated by the whore, harlot, 'veshya' image. Hence, the importance of the use of terminology like 'women in prostitution', instead of the commonly used term 'prostitute'. Women who practise prostitution use the term 'women in business' while referring to themselves. Now, after much discussion among ourselves, we have adopted the term people in prostitution and sex work (PPS) to include all persons who "make money out of sex".

This paper attempts to explore the violence of stigmatization that refuses to accept the reality of women in prostitution and sex work. It discusses community-based prostitution and sex work as experienced in the Indian context. In recent years this community has been fighting for a voice in all the debates about prostitution and sex work.

The 'Fallen Women' through History

The 'loose woman' has been the subject of much public discourse and debate, academic writing and policy making. In a similar way several perspectives have been articulated on such women. On one end of the spectrum is the view that prostitutes are victims of female sexual slavery. Kathleen Barry (1979), for instance, has elaborated on the manner in which prostitution is inherently violent, whether women are kidnapped, purchased, fraudulently contracted through organized crime syndicates or procured through love and befriending tactics.

This perspective, echoed by those working to end trafficking in women and children, assumes that all prostitutes are forced into the institution, and that making money from sex is synonymous with sexual exploitation. Complete abolition of prostitution is thus the logical solution to end such exploitation of women. This approach criminalizes the manifestations of sex work, such as soliciting, pimping, brothel-owning and trafficking, and often criminalizes the prostitute herself.

Interestingly, although prostitutes are considered to be victims, they are also viewed as wanton (liberated sexual beings), debauched (making 'valueless' money from sex) and morally weak. The whore stigma emphasized the 'evil' [sic] influence of such 'base' women on the 'good' moral character of society, deeming them 'deviant' women who transgressed the norms of 'acceptable' social behaviour. The concept of the fallen, debased and deviant woman has always governed public opinion, policy and law. Women have therefore been policed, coerced and raided, to be rescued, reformed and rehabilitated by a society that would like to order and control their lifestyles, regulate or abolish prostitution.

At the other end of the spectrum, spearheaded by prostitutes from associations such as COYOTE (Cast Off Your Old Tired Ethics) since the early 1970s, are those who argue that many adult women actually choose sex work as a viable option. Proponents of this approach view this voluntary decision to make money from sex as akin to selling other forms of labour. They contend that viewing prostitution as 'work' provides a basis for organizing to solve many of the problems of commercial sex. According to them, distinguishing sex work from other forms of labour reinforces the marginal, and therefore vulnerable status of the sex worker. Sex workers, they state, should then be entitled to labour rights and occupational health and safety regulations like all other workers. The assumption that sex work is a personal choice aims at complete de-criminalization of voluntary sex work and all related activities. Legalization of prostitution, demanded by some sex worker's groups, involves taking the subject outside the realm of criminal law, but advocates regulation of sex work through zoning and licensing laws.

Some associations of women in prostitution prefer use of the term 'commercial sex' instead of 'prostitution' or 'sex work' because these terms focus on the seller of sexual services and perhaps contribute to the invisibility of buyers. Yet, they point out that sex worker's priorities vary from one community to another. For example, improving health and safety standards in the workplace may be a realistic goal for those involved in a formal sex industry, but is not helpful for marginalized young people selling 'survival' sex spontaneously.

Critics of this approach, like Pateman (1989) claim that feminists who invoke "women's right to own their bodies" are reinforcing a language that can just as well validate their 'right' to sell their bodies through civil contracts for prostitution, surrogacy, marriage, labour or slavery. For Pateman, saying we "own our bodies" means and can only mean that we are 'free' to sell our bodies (our body parts or sexual or reproductive services) in the marketplace.

Prostitution for Pateman is the classic case of men as a 'fraternity' gaining a "right of access to women's bodies" through the fictive device of contract (voluntary consent). Underneath this contract is another, more insidious fiction that equates women's reproductive and sexual capacities with labour power, as a 'service' that can be alienated from the 'self' without compromising the self's 'moral freedom'. According to Pateman, "When a prostitute contracts out use of her body, she is doing something different from a worker getting a job; she is ... selling *herself* in a very real sense, alienating herself from her sexuality, which is integral to her 'womanhood".

A different approach to concepts like autonomy and self-ownership has been taken by feminists of colour in the United States, who are engaged in re-appropriating these concepts. Patricia Williams, for instance, is committed to reclaiming women's ownership of their flesh and blood by reinventing the language of self-ownership, or what she calls "the formulation of an autonomous social self" (Williams, 1995) . Those who tend, care for, carry are by definition those with authentic claims to be named owner of things or people whose growth they nurture. When the "objects of property" speak they remind us that the language of self-creation, self-propriety and freedom is always a story told and retold, and to reject that language wholesale is to leave those without property nothing at all to own. As Williams observes, to repudiate formalized claims to personal worth and rights is to trivialize the experience of those who historically have been treated as worthless. She argues that rather than discarding the rights discourse, we should expand and diversify it. The crucial function of the rights discourse – that of giving visibility to those previously invisible needs to be emphasized.

In recent years, the discourse around prostitution has changed and is now couched in the language of human rights.

Feminists, theorists and prostitutes' rights activists are involved in unravelling the complex and complicated world of sexual autonomy, free choice, sexual exploitation and agency versus victim debates. This discourse has helped in that it has shifted the focus from blaming the woman and her sexual life to a continuum ranging from the "beneficial exploitation of the institution of prostitution" to the "inherent victimisation of the woman in prostitution".

As Rajeshwari Sunder Rajan (in Ratna Kapoor, ed., 1996) observes, the prostitution question, "challenges us, as well, to ask whether prostitute interests are being truly represented in these debates. The urgency and force of the disagreements arise not only from the issues relating to prostitution, but also from the fact that the prostitution question has gathered around itself many of the issues that remain unresolved in feminism: the relationship between feminists and female victims of oppression; the construction of the female subject in terms of 'agency' (choice, autonomy, desire, voice); the public/private dimension of work/sexuality; the conceptualization of First World/Third World difference and sameness in women's status; the narrativization as progress of women's (here, especially, prostitutes') history.

Though the prostitutes' rights movement started in the late 1960s and early 70s, the rights approach has been challenged and will remain a dream as long as it is plagued by advocates of the moral brigade or the proponents of sexual autonomy and free choice, as mutually exclusive positions.

It is apparent that while the 'prostitution question' will be continued to be debated and arguments for and against, whether voluntary/forced, 'agency'/victim, trafficked/socialized, legal/cri minal, sexual slavery/sexual autonomy, exploited/liberated, will continue to occupy theorists, activists, and governments, prostitution as experienced by the women themselves is not given the kind of recognition it deserves in these debates. Unfortunately, the term 'trafficking' is being characterized solely by prostitution and is used synonymously with sexual exploitation. The term has acquired a moral value and is often seen to include not just procurement, sale and transport of women for the purposes of sex work, but sex work as well. For instance, though trafficking in human beings is covered under the Indian Constitution (Article 23), the primary target of the Immoral Trafficking Prevention Act (ITPA), 1986 is to punish immoral trafficking and traffickers. In practice, the ITPA ends up victimizing women in prostitution. There is an immediate need to redefine the term 'trafficking'. The definition must address the needs of all people, irrespective of gender, and must protect the rights of trafficked people. Failure to recognize their right to autonomy and self-determination will result only in repressive measures and restrictive policies.

Commercial sex was seen as an important public health issue throughout the 19th century. While concern about it declined in the 20th century due to improved management of sexually transmitted diseases and unwanted pregnancies, the HIV/AIDS epidemic has refuelled the concern. Public health once again dominates the way most societies deal with commercial sex. Legislation, public policy and widespread societal attitudes permeated by moral outrage, fail to recognize that there are complex dynamics at play which call for complex solutions. Most important, there is need to listen to those most affected – the women in prostitution.

The inability to accept that the movement for prostitutes' rights can be informed by the women in prostitution and sex workers themselves is as much a part of denial of human rights as discrimination of mainstream women on the basis of caste, class, race or religion. There is an immediate need to unravel and reach out and listen to the women in the communities.

The present discourse fails to recognize the dynamics of an institution that encompasses a wide spectrum of elements from violence and exploitation on the one hand, and autonomy and agency to choose the best possible options, on the other. Prostitution is a way of life. While it is true that all women are not victims, to believe that all women are there out of free choice is also utopian.

Unfortunately, the dominant discourse does not identify the day-to-day struggles much less the strength of a minority community comprised mainly of women who face the brutal and criminalized world they inhabit. It is a struggle that is fortified by a socialization that encourages and strengthens their ability to deal with a hostile and violent environment. Communities of people in prostitution and sex work have repeatedly scorned the attempts of mainstream patriarchal society to control, regulate and abolish the institution of prostitution.

A VAMP statement declares: "We believe that a woman's sexuality is an integral part of her as a woman, as varied as her mothering, domestic and such other skills. We do not believe that sex has a sacred space and women who have sex for reasons other than its reproductive importance are violating this space. Or if they chose to make money from the transaction, they are immoral or debauched."

The Violence of Stigmatization

Stigmatization, which has its roots in the standards set by patriarchal morality, is experienced as the major factor that prevents women from accessing their rights. This impacts the lives of women in more ways than one. Some of the rights denied to women due to discrimination are: freedom from physical and mental abuse and the right to education and information, health care, housing, social security and welfare services.

The most basic of all is the denial of the right to practise the 'business of making money from sex'. "We protest against a society that deems us immoral and illegal mainly because we do not accept its mores, rules and governance. We protest against the various forces of mainstream society that deny us the right to liberty, security, fair administration of justice, respect for our lives, discrimination, freedom of expression and association," declares the VAMP statement succinctly.

It is the *randi* (whore) stigma that pushes women in prostitution outside the rights framework, effectively cutting them off from privileges and rights supposedly accorded to all citizens, irrespective of what they do for a living. Women in prostitution and sex work from VAMP state that, "As people who experience violence as a part of our daily lives, we are being more and more penalised by increasing violence in a society that is trying to order and control our lifestyles. As women in prostitution, we protest against a society that forces on us the violence of a judgmental attitude".

Health Care

Accessing health care is a major concern for women in prostitution and sex work. While the 'immoral whore' image makes it very difficult to get good medical treatment, illiteracy, ignorance and fear of the medical establishment renders them open to exploitation and extortion of money and resources.

Reproduced here are responses regarding health care by women in prostitution and sex work from West Bengal, Orissa, Andhra Pradesh, Karnataka, Maharashtra, Tamil Nadu, Kerala and the Union Territories of Goa and Pondicherry from a report prepared by the National Commission for Women:

(a) Medical and paramedical staff at government hospitals have a callous, indifferent and often humiliating attitude. Irrelevant and embarrassing questions about sexual positions etc. are often asked.
(b) Forced free sex with doctors and social workers is commonplace.
(c) Doctors often refuse treatment and admit women to hospital claiming that they are AIDS carriers.
(d) In many centres doctors make the peons and attendants conduct the physical examination and only then treat the women.

Unfortunately, the HIV/AIDS epidemic has singled out people in prostitution and sex work as "carriers and vectors of spread of HIV". Apart from the stigma already attached to their work, society has further marginalized them as core transmitters of HIV infection. It fails to recognize that they are but links in the broad networks of heterosexual transmission of HIV. Women in prostitution and sex work constitute a community that bears and will continue to bear the greatest impact of the HIV epidemic in India, suffering high levels of infection and re-infection.

Propagating the myth that women in prostitution and sex work are core transmitters of HIV serves the purpose of 'prostitution bashers' imbued with the moral and judgmental attitude that reinforces the prejudice that AIDS is an 'impure' disease which afflicts immoral and evil persons. The net result is to further target the women which

(a) increases public and police violence against them;

(b) decreases their ability to assert themselves;
(c) allows customers to demand and force unsafe sex upon them;
(d) increases the rate of HIV among women, customers and the families of the customers; and
(e) denies them access to health care services.

The role of women in prostitution and sex work in HIV/AIDS prevention is little acknowledged. In fact, it is now well recognized that women in prostitution are the best educators of their male clients.

Criminalization: The Brutalization of People in Prostitution

Being women in prostitution puts them into a caste-class of their own. This caste-class occupies the lowest rung in the hierarchy and is structured 'outside' the hierarchy, as we know it. Mobility therefore is almost impossible and then only through deceit and/or money. The need to protect family members, especially children from this stigma, is an everyday struggle. Like Bandawwa Makadwale from VAMP said, "all the money we have earned cannot help us to live in peace. The outside world pushes us out and does not even accept our children who are not in the business of making money out of sex. We are unable to ensure the happiness of our children. Our health and our children suffer the most due to this stigma and discrimination."

For instance, the initial baseline survey of the community in Sangli in 1992, done by SANGRAM, showed that less than 2 per cent of the women have ever been to school of any kind and less than half of this reached high school. Though most of the children are going to school, the baseline shows a very high dropout rate, especially after primary school. As Vijay Kamble of Miraj says, "It is very painful to listen to your peers make snide remarks about your own mother. When my own teacher came to the community for sex, I ran and ran till I was breathless. I was so frightened. I never went back to school."

There are many reasons for the high dropout rate, ranging from experiencing the educational system as hostile to them as children of women in prostitution, to an inability to pass school examinations. This hostility continues to hound their interactions with the mainstream, whatever the milieu in which this interaction takes place. For instance, Renuka, who has studied up to master's degree in commerce, left her job in a local bank because the manager took to calling her in to ask questions about her mother and the other women in the community.

Prostitution as Experienced by Women

This section presents the narratives, collected by activists of VAMP – a collective of five thousand women in prostitution and sex work in Central India.

The patterns that emerged through the stories included a sense of economic power as the female head of the household, monetary gain, economic stability and security, a feeling of liberation from constricting social norms and anger due to the feeling of powerlessness against the intolerance of mainstream society and its judgmental attitude. Women who had a chance to leave have chosen to remain, accepting that prostitution, as a way of life, is a better option than the double standards that exist in mainstream society. They have chosen the option to leave only when found convenient (and re-enter) depending on the circumstances that dictated their decisions.

Moralistic and Sacred Sex

The narratives also depict a sense of trivialization of the entire sexual act into a matter-of-fact occurrence. Apprawa *mausi* – a big gharwali (brothel owner) – said, "Men come to us regularly not just for sex but to experience the freedom from rigid, moral and sacred social norms. Wives are sacred and/or refuse to be fun and girl friends may demand far greater returns."

Negativism and Criminalization

The narratives also brought out the fact that it is the increasing violence of negativity regarding women in prostitution and prostitution *per se*, that forces women in prostitution to operate under the absolute criminalization of their work/business. 'Protection' –

the overt armour that prostitution is encased within becomes a must, thus the brothel owner-pimp-*malak*-police-criminal nexus is almost impossible to avoid.

Increase in criminalization with the inevitable policing by the state and its law enforcement machinery contributes to increasing brutality in prostitution. For instance, this is clearly visible in the difference that the metropolis makes to the practice of prostitution. Mumbai and its (in) famous 'cages', Kolkata and its red-light glitter as compared to the relaxed atmosphere of Sangli, Kolhapur, Miraj, Barshi – the small townships, needs to be seen to be believed. Also, women in townships where the crime rate in the general population is higher like Solapur, Ichalkaranji and Karad, face more brutalization and violence, though not as drastic as is seen in Mumbai or Delhi, the bigger metros. Increase in criminalization is proportional to the increase in brutality, violence, abuse, debt bondage, deception, coercion, and slavery-like practice within prostitution.

Madhuri Sawant, a woman in prostitution, who was trafficked to Mumbai from Miraj relates the horrifying manner in which she was forced to accept conditions of abuse, being caged in a small room without ventilation, not allowed to talk to her colleagues, service clients that pimps brought to the room, not have the choice to deny a client etc. She felt she had relinquished her life to the trafficker and madam. After her escape, she said, "It is because Mumbai is so big and frightening that I felt alone and helpless. I thought that the *dalal* from Mumbai would treat me like a human being but he was ruthless. So, many girls are brought to Miraj but we never treat them with such disrespect for their wishes. Even a woman like me, who had ten years experience in prostitution and sex work, could not deal with the *goondas* in Mumbai. What must be happening to new, young girls? They must be really brutalized."

Legal repression, as a direct result of moralistic criminalization by the state, has been exercised from time immemorial to control and regulate prostitution. Women in prostitution and sex work are made to believe that they are in an 'illegal' business. This interpretation of the law, which the police state forces on the women, allows the *goonda* elements to use the site of prostitution and sex work to practise their illegal, criminal activity, depending on the vulnerability of the women, resulting in an uneasy alliance between the state, the criminals and the women.

Children in Prostitution

The increasing demand for and supply of children into prostitution is also a direct result of the helplessness that is experienced by families from the mainstream and communities of women in prostitution, who are lured and exploited by this criminal nexus. Be it through abduction, kidnap, coercion or even willingness of the family to use their very young as a financial resource. That children in prostitution are abused, physically, sexually and mentally raped is evident from the stories and anecdotes that women recount of their own past lives. The sense of helplessness and anger that women in prostitution face as mothers has been recorded in numerous instances. Women react not to 'making money from sex' *per se* but to the violence they experience within the institution of prostitution.

Retirement

Retirement could be voluntary or forced. The age factor is very important. As the women grow older, they loose their clients to younger girls. Gradually retirement from business becomes a traumatic reality. The *gharwali* (madam) is also a result of this process wherein the woman chooses to remain in business as a manager of a brothel.

Marriage is also a major reason for women to retire from business. Sometimes, this is temporary and they re-enter business if things do not work out. Some women who live with a man for a short or long period may choose to remain in business or retire completely.

Departure

Forced 'rehabilitation', raids by the police, violence and social repression also contribute to women leaving business. Well-meaning social activists also abuse the women by using punitive action to 'rescue' and 'rehabilitate' women and children in prostitution. Punitive action with the help of an abusive and corrupt law enforcement machinery creates an atmosphere of fear, repression and suppression that helps to drive the entire process underground. In some cases, this process could lead to retirement from business.

Women have also been known to depart from prostitution by running away and making a life outside prostitution/sex work, wherein they gain 'respectability' by the denial of their past life, or by being 'kept' by a benefactor, sometimes grown up children take over responsibilities, and more often than not health reasons make them drop out of business totally.

Trafficking/Migration for the Purpose of Sex Work with relation to HIV Vulnerability

Trafficking by definition implies the use of coercion, deception, abuse and assault. This could mean that women in trafficked situations might suffer critical health problems. For women who are trafficked into the sex trade, the problem is a very real threat. It is compounded by the inability to access immediate treatment service for STDs or related problems. In situations of abuse enforcement of condom use is not possible.

Undoubtedly, women who have been trafficked are more vulnerable than men and more likely to be in a situation where they are unable to control and protect themselves from HIV transmission. As illegal migrants engaged in an illegal trade, they are very often subjected to sexual abuse in the hands of authorities, including immigration and police officials, whose systematic involvement in the trafficking trade is well known and documented. Forcible detention, lack of access to redressal, corruption in police administration and invisibility ensure that women rights can be violated, controlled and abused. Given the fact that HIV transmission is most efficient in situations of repression and abuse, women in trafficked situations are more vulnerable and at a greater risk of contracting HIV.

A ray of hope is offered by small NGOs in most countries in the region that are struggling with the problem of HIV vulnerability in trafficked persons, but these are scattered responses.

The common perception prevails in the society that it is the trafficked person who is responsible for their own fate also contributes to social and political apathy towards issues that affect HIV transmission in this group. It is almost impossible to expect that trafficked person who fears repatriation will access treatment and services for HIV.

NGOs working with trafficked people work/operate in hostile conditions. Building the confidence and trust of trafficked persons is not an easy task. As 'stateless' people without papers, trafficked persons prefer being invisible and underground. If they are women in prostitution and sex work even more so because prostitution in most countries is illegal and it is almost impossible to access women who are under the 'protection' of the criminal nexus and trafficking syndicates. Fear of police and legal repression is also a major reason why women shy away from outreach workers.

Unfortunately, a comprehensive documentation of groups working in this field is very limited. While there are many groups that work with trafficked women and illegal migrants, they are very few who actually offer services for HIV/AIDS prevention, care and support. Many women's groups in sending and receiving countries provide services and support to women who are victims of trafficking, but HIV/AIDS prevention and education is not part of their agenda.

The problem is compounded by the contradictions and lacunae in the management of the HIV/AIDS epidemic in the countries of the region. Short. project-oriented interventions with a targeted approach cannot hope to achieve a sustained response to the epidemic. In situations wherein access to treatment services to the general population is itself difficult and sporadic, a service for vulnerable groups is an almost impossible dream. Programmes that view women in sex work as a means to reaching the sexually active male population, rather than the sex worker themselves, are doomed from the start. Most governments in the region resort to such targeted interventions. The targeted approach therefore is proving to be an alienating process that will continue to blame marginalized communities rather than empower them to combat HIV. In such a situation, it is inevitable that the control and implementation of such programmes will always remain with the implementing agencies, rather than owned by the communities.

Voices from Underground

One of the most valuable lessons learned during the course of our work has been to listen to the women, and respect their wisdom earned from a life of resistance. As activist Durga Pujari from VAMP put it, "Over the years, we have become 'commercial sex workers' from 'common prostitutes', debates are held about us and we are discussed in documents, covenants and declarations. The problem however is that when we try to inform the arguments our stories are disbelieved and we are treated as if we cannot comprehend our own lives. Thus, we are either romanticized, victimized, or worse and our reality gets buried and distorted."

The labour/sex work story limits prostitution as a site of work. This is at variance with the communities of women in prostitution who have through the ages lived the life of being prostitutes, whores, *veshyas* or *dandhewalis*. Prostitution thus cannot be reduced simply to work, since it depicts a way of life accepted by the communities in a continuum from pre-initiation to retirement. Prostitution, like marriage and family, which also control women's sexuality, is not a monolithic institution. The degree of autonomy possible, the extent of abuse and violence and the possibility of accessing rights vary widely according to the situation. Women experience the institution of prostitution in a complex way, negotiating spaces and struggling for survival.

The women in prostitution are survivors with the sharpest insights – be it on the "double standards of morality" in society, the violent intricate underpinnings of trafficking networks that are brutalizing prostitution or even the hollowness of state sponsored rights which strengthen the violators more than the violated. And, it is these insights that will best define the contours of a rights discourse that will help resist the violence in their lives marginalized by the hypocrisies of the 'system'. Like all survivors, they have the courage and strength to create a world that has much to offer – a world touched not only by their pain but also their dream for a society and a people who will affirm their right to self worth, dignity and livelihood that no one agency can either give or deny.

References

Agustin, Laura et al. 1999. 'The Sex Sector: A Victory for Diversity: A Perspective on the ILO Recommendations', Women's Global Network for Reproductive Rights Newsletter No. 2/3.

Barry, Kathleen. 1979. *Female Sexual Slavery.* Prentice-Hall, Inc.

Centre for Feminist Legal Research. 1999. 'Memorandum on Reform of Laws Relating to Prostitution in India'. New Delhi.

National Commission for Women. 1997. 'Societal Violence Against Women and Children in Prostitution'. NCW, New Delhi.

Overs, Cheryl and Paulo Longo. 1997. 'Making Sex Work Safe', Network of Sex Work Projects, London.

Pateman, Carole. 1989. *The Disorder Women: Democracy, Feminism and Political Theory.* Cambridge: Polity Press.

Petchesky, R.P. 1999. 'The Body as Property: A Feminist Re-vision'. *In* SANGRAM. 'Of Veshyas, Vamps, Whores and Women'.

Sunder Rajan, Rajeshwari. 1996. 'The Prostitution Questions(s): Female Agency, Sexuality and Work'. *In* Ratna Kapoor (ed.) *Feminist Terrains in Legal Domains: Interdisciplinary Essays on Women and Law in India.*

VAMP-Veshya AIDS Muqabala Parishad. 1996. 'A Statement of Women in Prostitution'.

Williams, Patricia J. 1995. *The Rooster's on the Persistence of Prejudice,* USA: Harvard University Press.

6

Location and Articulation of Reproductive and Sexual Rights

Whose Rights? Whose Claims?

MEENA GOPAL

This paper explores the location of reproductive and sexual rights within the human rights discourse. Reproductive and sexual rights, which have emerged in discussions and campaigns around women's health, and subsequently into the discourse of women's rights, are human rights. They have been advanced as some of the initial rights specific to women. They continue to be addressed in combination and this is seen to be problematic in clarifying both reproductive and/or sexual rights of women and rights of sexuality minorities. For example, while reproductive rights are associated with issues of women's bodily integrity, the concept of sexual rights delimits an understanding of sexuality, which goes much beyond women's rights. It marginalizes a range of people whose gender identities and sexualities fall outside the claim of sexual rights as defined under the rubric of health rights. In this paper, the debate around the claims and campaigns of both these rights using a human rights, framework, is discussed. In addition, it also addresses the problem associated with combining both the sets of rights. The problem arises due to the locations from which they are articulated. In conclusion, the paper urges for a re-articulation of the rights from sites that actually empower the groups whose claims are advanced rather than their rights being appropriated or marginalized.

Place of Reproductive and Sexual Rights in the Human Rights Discourse

It is the efforts of the international feminist and women's health discourse that have foregrounded reproductive and sexual rights of women within the human rights framework. The concept of reproductive health was born out of a persistent and desperate need on part of women health activists and advocates to change the population control approach of development thinkers and actors of the 1960s and 1970s. Their campaigns have had to focus on women's reproductive sexuality and reproductive potential to direct their advancement of women's human rights. They opposed the overall rationale of states that population control in the social interest has a higher place over individual well-being and individual rights. There was a significant difference between the women's groups' campaigns in the countries of the North (developed) and the South (less developed). Most of them, while campaigning for better conditions of life and health for women, were also reacting to and opposing state anti-natalist or pro-natalist measures targeting women and demanding more sensitive policies and programmes for women's well-being and respecting their rights. In Asia, women's health activism has been largely in response to authoritarian population control policies of the governments as in India, or in access to abortion and contraceptive choice as in Phillipines.[1]

As a result of agreements at the International Conference on Population and Development at Cairo in 1994, reproductive rights have been classified as an integral part of human rights and therefore subject to international law. There is a reluctance on part of states and international agencies to intervene in traditionally defined 'family matters' and act against gender-based violations of human rights, especially as they have been proved to most frequently occur in the supposedly private realms of the family, reproduction and sexuality. The feminists working from a population and development paradigm, speak of a model of reproductive and sexual rights for women's empowerment, which requires the presence of enabling conditions. These include the availability of health services, access issues, finance, support systems, etc., which should be the responsibility of the state and other mediating institutions. Further, they advocate an ethical framework which stresses respect for bodily integrity, personhood, equality and diversity in women's lives.[2]

Despite all this, there is still a lack of recognition and acceptance of reproductive and sexual rights as part of political or economic and socio-cultural rights. Reproductive health requires moving beyond the biomedical model to examine health in its social context, addressing social determinants, including gender, of health and ill-health so that interventions can be appropriately designed.[3] However, since these interventions are designed on an already constructed programme geared to population control, they continue to stress the physical aspects of health. Further, despite claiming that empowerment of women should be an end in itself, the overwhelming stress on quantitative goals continue. The overriding goal seems to be population stabilization, while women's health seems to have only an instrumentalist value.

Problems of Advocating for Reproductive and Sexual Rights from the Reproductive Health Framework

The International Conference on Population and Development articulated the concept of reproductive health in a manner that boosted the efforts of women's health advocates, who have been leading the campaign for protection and promotion of women's right to their body and reproductive decision-making. Many of these were women activists from the North and who wield considerable influence in international forums. This group perceives that the population policy of a country should be part of a broader approach to overall women's health, and they place reproductive health within this broad spectrum of humane population policies. They examine the ethical bases of the current population policies, and say that a gender perspective will transform population policies to reflect a commitment to ethics and human rights, and that such a policy can be effective if it just does not focus on fertility control, but is designed as part of human development to create an enabling environment within which people can attain their health and rights.[4] The problem is that reproductive rights are severely compromised as the articulation of reproductive health is within an already existent programme geared to population control.

That apart, reproductive rights as right to bodily integrity has a longer history in the birth control movement. While feminists and socialists were among the first advocates for birth control, there were numerous other actors, such as the Malthusians and neo-Malthusians, who had an interest in advocating birth control, especially to the working class in England, in order to reduce their poverty. In the United States, it was the socialists, particularly the Owenites, who spearheaded the movement for birth control on the basis of it being a right of women to control their bodies and sexuality. They also clarified that the cause of poverty was not overpopulation but unequal distribution of wealth. The movement for birth control also attracted women radicals, who extended the concept of birth control, taking it into the arena of sexuality while separating it from reproduction. They utilized the issue of birth control to advocate women's rights by making it a pre-condition for individual freedom. Many of these women radicals were also active in the working class rebellions in the United States. Emma Goldman, an anarchist and Margaret Sanger, a socialist, were the important leaders of the birth control movement in the US. In several European countries, such as France, Holland and Germany, birth control was the demand of political activists. The movement weakened later due to the moving away of the socialists from women's concerns, and the waning of radicalism in the pre-war years. In the post-World War I era, a new set of actors entered to fill the gap left by the radicals: the eugenicists and professionals, mainly doctors. Several liberal doctors publicly supported as long as they were given the monopoly of prescription of contraceptives, even demanding legislation for it. These trends shifted the movement from focusing on birth control as a larger social issue to its regulation. The other entrants into the birth control movement – the eugenicists – advocated compulsory sterilization for the poor who were deemed genetically inferior, and hence requiring curbing of their capacity to breed.[5]

In India, social reformers like R.D. Karve had attempted to introduce sex education and reproductive awareness for women. Karve published a monthly called *Samaj Swasthya* and ran a dispensary and counselling centre for this purpose. Another reformer who advocated women's liberation, Keshav Kumar Thakur in his book in Hindi, *Navin Dampatya Jeevan Mein Striyon Ka Adhikar*, writes about women's health and education. He says, "Freedom is essential for the development of health and education. If there is no freedom neither can health measures be successful nor will education be capable of upliftment in life. Life can develop only in freedom" (cited in Chayanika, 1999: 17–18).[6] The influence of the birth control movement was also felt in other parts of India, and is evident in the writings of Periyar E.V. Ramaswamy Naicker of the Dravidian movement in the early 20th century in South India. In his *Penn Yen Adimaiaanaal* (Why Women were Enslaved?), challenging the naturalised idea of motherhood in Hindu society, Periyar wrote that birth control for women was one of the preconditions for women's liberation.[7]

Feminists who have all along struggled for reproductive rights of women, particularly with reference to bodily integrity, given the long history of women's right to birth control, suddenly find that the rhetoric of reproductive rights has been appropriated by the population control lobby. Even though Malthusianism evolved with Reverend Thomas Malthus' famous dictum of attributing all social problems to population growth, especially of the poor, and advocating population control as the solution to all these problems, today neo-Malthusian policy makers subscribe to this view and look to the 'contraceptive revolution' through state-directed family planning programmes as the solution. What the neo-Malthusian analysts have succeeded in is the co-option of the feminist tenet of individual choice in reproduction, they have appropriated and emphasized women's reproductive rights as the rationale for family planning interventions. Their role along with those of women's rights advocates emerged as a consensus in the Programme of Action at the Cairo Conference.[8] As the current discourse on reproductive health stands, it only represents claims to protect the rights of women as child bearers, while the advocates of population control mouth the need for women to have both reproductive and sexual rights so that it 'contributes' to population stabilization, reduction of poverty and thereby to sustainable development.

Viewing reproductive health care as a subset of health care needs of women is also confounded by the fact that in most countries reproductive health care is only a different nomenclature for family planning services. The logical outcome of this approach is that women's health is viewed within the domain of control over reproduction, and women end up as targets of population control. Thus, the link between reproductive choice and population control becomes sealed.

Feminists have also been emphatic about the need to distinguish between health and family planning, as the ideology behind family planning is control those who consume, while general health needs of women remain unaddressed. Within the population control approach, which was influenced by the Malthusian paradigm of too many people competing for too few resources, the stress was on perceiving women as breeders of too many children and therefore constructing programmes that would curb their fertility by whatever means. These feminists, in India for example, state their case from the experience of societal and state control of women's bodies through coercive population policies in the name of fertility regulation. They also state the need to counter Malthusianism with the historical fact of depletion of resources from the less developed and poorer countries and the current patterns of consumption and expenditure in the developed nations which contribute to the equation of resources and population. What this position states is the need for a sane and sensible development policy and a health policy that will ensure the empowerment of women.[9] All of this discussion has focused on reproductive and sexual rights, however limited they may be, in a very gendered manner, reflecting only women's concerns. However, there are a whole gamut of people who continue to be fought for rights, under the rubric of sexual rights. There are various contentious issues related to their articulation. Some of these are attempted to be examined in the next section.

The Problem of Conjoining Sexual Rights with Reproductive Rights

Claims to sexual rights, fortunately or unfortunately, have emerged from women's reproductive rights advocacy. Reproductive rights has gained some global acceptance, and it uses some of the powerful aspects of the health and human rights paradigm (embracing both promotional and protective approaches) and puts rights claims within the broader social justice movements. It also addresses the social and material conditions of race, class and other aspects of identity as they impact reproductive rights.

However, there are problems in conjoining sexual with reproductive rights, as it marginalizes the rights of sexual minorities, whose sexuality falls both outside of the dominant heteronormativity,[10] as well as concerned with reproductive potentiality. However, the conflation of sexual rights has caused it to be viewed as a subset of reproductive rights, with a less developed articulation. This has caused the invisibility of an array of people of varying ages and non-conforming sexual identities, as well as non-reproductive sexual practices, neglecting men as rights holders, and leaving many marginalized people (such as lesbian, gay, bisexual and transgender people, or broadly queer[11] people) outside the framework of human rights protection in the context of sexual behaviour. Sexual rights are the claim of only married heterosexual people, especially women. The removal of non-heterosexual, non-procreative sexual activities from human rights protection has to be surrendered to moral, religious, medical or criminal regulation. Hence, such persons should be named and recognized and brought within the circle of rights protection.[12] Such a framework of protection has also to incorporate contemporary theories of the social construction of sexuality. Sexual values and erotic conduct are always in a flux and conflicts and disputes over them become vehicles to displace social anxiety, especially during great social upheavals and social stress.[13]

It has to be acknowledged that the global pandemic of HIV/AIDS and the need to respond to it has focused new attention to sexuality in the field of public health. In recent times human rights strategies have been looked upto analyse ways that restrict or empower persons in developing and enjoying their sexualities. Some of the legal claims internationally, regarding (homo)sexual conduct and identity, have cited the rights to protection from invasions of privacy and protection from discrimination.

Another major force that exhorts the usage of the human rights framework to advance rights of sexuality minorities or queer people are the numerous political assertions centering around sexuality – the numerous lesbian and gay rights movements, movements for rights of transgender people, etc.[14] In India, the rights of queer people remain unrecognized as the movement is still struggling against a lack of social acceptance, the simultaneously existence of queer invisibility (as normal people) and hyper-visibility (as deviant and abnormal), the silencing that goes on due to fear of discovery of one's sexuality, and the continuous violation of basic rights by the laws, the police, family, media, popular culture, workspaces, public spaces, and household spaces. However, even as the law has been complicit in violation of rights, it still remains a tool and a language that could be used to question the denial of rights.

At international level the Bill of Rights has no mention of the rights of queer people. It is only in 1991 that the Amnesty International re-interpreted its mandate to consider prisoners of conscience, i.e., persons arrested for their homosexual identity or for engaging in consensual homosexual activity in private, despite considerable internal opposition. There has been a progressive internationalization that has been achieved by the use of quasi-judicial procedures/bodies to litigate for rights of queer people (such as the UN Human Rights Committee) and using international law to advocate for rights of queer people.[15] While silence around the sexual rights of queer people denies them rights-based claims to information on sexuality, for conditions of safety and the respect for diversity, and for the enabling conditions needed for enjoyment of sexual rights, it also wipes out a range of non-procreative sexual behaviours of heterosexual people too. It also fails to address rights of sex workers, or others engaging in consensual sex of any sort and who are punished.

The contention is whether sexual rights and the discussions around sexuality have to be articulated along with or independent of reproductive rights. The resolution lies in having cross-cultural and cross-sectoral coalitions that are strategic in tackling states.

Conclusion

Thus, both at a conceptual level as well as at the level of claiming reproductive or sexual rights, in the form of legal recognition or services for care and protection, there is need for a re-articulation of the specific rights. Therefore, this review has highlighted the fallacy of addressing reproductive and sexual rights in combination, so that the rights of all concerned are articulated effectively and attained. It also underlines the necessity of positing the rights specifically from diverse locations, where one right does not override the other.

Notes

1. Claudia Garcia-Moreno and Amparo Claro, 'Challenges from the Women's Health Movement: Women's Rights versus Population Control', in Gita Sen, Adrienne Germain, and Lincoln C. Chen (eds.), *Population Policies Reconsidered: Health. Empowerment and Rights*, IWHC and Harvard Center for Population and Development Studies, Boston, 1994; Jonathan Mann and Sofia Gruskin, 'Women's Health and Human Rights: Genesis of the Health and Human Rights Movement,' Editorial, *Health and Human Rights* (an international quarterly journal) Vol. 1, No. 4, pp. 309–313.
2. Sonia Correa and Rosalind Petchesky, 'Reproductive and Sexual Rights: A Feminist Perspective', in Gita Sen et al. (eds.), ibid.
3. Gita Sen et al. (eds.), Ibid.
4. Ibid.
5. Betsy Hartmann, *Reproductive Rights and Wrongs: The Global Politics of Population Control*, Revised Edition (I Edition: 1987, Harper and Row: New York) South End Press, Boston, 1995.
6. Chayanika, Swatija and Kamaxi, 'The Family Planning Programme: From Planning to Control', in *We and Our Fertility: The Politics of Technological Intervention*, Mumbai, 1999.

7. Geetha, V. and S.V. Rajadurai, *Towards a Non-Brahmin Millennium: From Iyothee Das to Periyar*, Samya Publications, 1998.
8. Asoka Bandarage, *Women, Population and Global Crisis: A Political-Economic Analysis,* Zed Books, London, 1997.
9. Chayanika, et al., ibid; Hartmann, ibid.
10. Heteronormativity implies a normative system of belief and practices where binary constructions (of say, male and female sexes), complement each other. In sexual relations, the normative framework only recognizes heterosexual relations, considering as abnormal or deviant, same-sex relationships.
11. Queer connotes all marginalized sexualities, such as lesbian, gay, bisexual, transgender, *hijra, kothi,* etc. Since the list of gender categories could be exhaustive given the fluidity of gender identities and sexual preferences, the term queer is used to connote the category of people encompassed.
12. Alice M. Miller, 'Sexual but not Reproductive: Exploring the Junction and Disjunction of Sexual and Reproductive Rights', *Health and Human Rights* an international quarterly journal, Vol. 4, No. 2, pp. 69–109.
13. Gayle Rubin, 'Thinking Sex: Notes for a Radical Theory for a Politics of Sexuality', in Carol Vance (ed.), *Pleasure and Danger: Exploring Female Sexuality*, London: Pandora Press, 1992.
14. Charlotte Bunch and Claudia Hinojosa, *Lesbians Travel the Roads of Feminism Globally*, Mexico, 2000; Arvind Narrain, *Queer: Despised Sexuality, Law and Social Change*, Books for Change, Bangalore, 2004; Bina Fernandez (ed.), *Humjinsi: A Resource Book on Lesbian, Gay and Bisexual Rights in India,* India Centre for Human Rights and Law, Mumbai, 1999; PUCL-Karnataka, *Human Rights Violations against the Transgender Community: A Study of Kothi and Hijra Sex Workers in Bangalore, India*, September 2003.
15. Arvind Narrain, 2004, (Ibid) pp. 15–24.

7

Reproductive Health Rights and Gender Bias

Perceptions of Rural Women

ANJALI KULKARNI

Indian Constitution has given equal rights to its all citizens and it recognizes that there would not be discrimination based on the caste, religion and sex. Still, in reality, it is found that the women's status is secondary in society. It gets reflected through various development indicators. Health is one of the important indicators that throw light on society's attitudes towards women. Declining sex ratio, increasing number of sex-selective abortions, declining nutritional status of women of all age groups, and alarming rates of violence against women are some issues of concern.

The women are always perceived as the 'producers' of the children' and the policy planners also have given undue importance to this role, but it is always forgotten that the women have also other health problems, related to the reproductive health. In the race of achieving the targets of the family planning operations the women are becoming 'cases'. They are cared only if they are 'cases'. The present health services do not provide effectively for these other health problems. Instead of making the services more need-based due to pressure of globalization process, there is privatization of the health services. As a result of the globalization process, there is also feminization of poverty and women are left without resources. This forces them to remain without treatment in case of illness, as they are not able to afford the private sources and there are varieties of barriers in using the present government services. This pushes women in unending morbidities.

In this context of increasing privatization and globalization, it is important to understand women's perceptions about their health rights and gender bias they face. This would facilitate for women's empowerment for their own health.

The present paper is based on two qualitative studies conducted by Rural Campus, Tata Institute of Social Sciences (TISSRC), Mumbai. In these studies the women from drought-prone area had participated. This paper presents women's experiences about family planning, the health seeking behaviour and their access to food. The paper also presents the empowerment modules developed by TISSRC.

Reproductive Health Rights and Gender Bias

The area of reproductive health includes both men and women. But reproductive health rights of men and women need to be talked separately. Especially in the Indian culture the women's reproductive rights need to be discussed as the women are considered secondary and there is strong hold of deep-rooted patriarchal thoughts in all spheres of the life. The women's bodies are perceived as the machines for child bearing and rearing. The women's bodies are controlled for several reasons and there are social and religious sanctions for the same. The women are targeted for the population control. They are not perceived as the human beings and are treated as the 'objects'. They do not participate in policy making and also are not decision-makers in their personal lives. Thus, there is need to safeguard their interests.

Now, a question arises: What are reproductive health rights? In 1968, at Teheran Conference, it was for the first time that the delegates attempted to define reproductive health rights. But, after that till the International Conference on Population and Development (ICPD) in 1994, there was not much discussion on the reproductive rights of the individuals. This conference developed the contents of the reproductive health rights. It stated that the reproductive rights go hand in hand of certain human rights, which were already recognized, by the forums like United

Nations etc. These rights are based on the recognition of the basic right of all the couples and individuals to decide freely and responsibly the number, spacing and timing of their children and to have the information and means to do so to attain the highest standard of sexual and reproductive sexual health. It also includes the right to make decisions concerning reproduction free of discrimination, coercion and violence as expressed in human rights documents. The important feature of the IPCD is that it brought the women's health to the centre stage and linked it to the development issues. It was also instrumental in broadening the concept of development to emphasize on a sustainable, equity-oriented model of development. Such a model recognized that health of people depended on equitable distribution of power and resources and that people's participation was a key to achieving equity and sustainability in all aspects of life.

Further, the Beijing Conference (1995) continued the IPCD thoughts on reproductive rights directly into the Platform of Action. It states that "good health is essential to leading a productive and fulfilling life and the right of all women to control all aspects of their health, in particular their own fertility, is basic to their empowerment. It further states that the human rights of women include their right to have control over and decide freely and responsibly on matters related to their sexuality, including sexual and reproductive health, free of coercion, discrimination and violence".

In 1999 Article 12 of Convention on the Elimination of All Forms of Discrimination Against Women (CEDAW) clearly stated women's rights regarding health. It recognized access to health care, including reproductive health as a basic right. It includes interventions at preventive level as well as the treatment of diseases and conditions affecting women. It further says that the state should ensure universal access for all women to a full range of high quality and affordable health care, including sexual and reproductive health services.

Thus, the reproductive rights of women not only include the rights on their own bodies, and freedom to decide the time and number of children, but to get good health services also, which would cater to their health problems, and all women should have access to these services.

Against this backdrop we now analyze what rural women say about their reproductive rights. As already stated, the discussion is based on two qualitative studies conducted in 2001 and 2003 by the TISSRC, Mumbai. Among these, the first one, "An Exploratory Study on Women's Health in Rural Maharashtra" (also referred to as Rural Women Study) adopted the life/developmental cycle approach. The women in the age group 11–45 years, who were mainly at three stages, i.e., adolescence, young adulthood (marriage and child bearing) and menopause, were covered. In all 400 women from two villages in Tuljapur block of Osmanabad district, Marathwada region of Maharashtra participated in the study. The study had focused on women's illnesses, and social, cultural and political factors associated with these illnesses. The special efforts were made to understand the health seeking process and the factors inhibiting the same. The agriculture was the main source of employment and the women from all caste groups were covered in the study. The illiteracy rate was quite high.

The second study, "Social Assessment of Reproductive and Child Health Programme: Osmanabad Urban" (referred to as Social RCH Study) was a part of national level study conducted by Tata Institute of Social Sciences. A total of 320 women and men beneficiaries of this major health programme participated in this study. The study also focused on issues like health rights, social and gender equity.

The beneficiaries who participated in the study were drawn from lower socio-economic classes. Majority depended on the daily wages (mainly form-based activities) and petty self-employment activities. The literacy levels were very low and the majority of women were illiterate.

Osmanabad is one of the undeveloped districts in the Maharashtra. Agriculture is the main source of employment and there is no industrial development. It comes in the drought-prone belt and recurrent drought is a common phenomenon. Migration, unemployment leading to poverty and child marriages are major social problems. It also has poorly developed infrastructure in terms of roads, railways and transport facilities. It is very caste sensitive in nature and culturally strongly male dominated.

Women's Perceptions regarding Health Rights and Gender Bias

The qualitative nature of the studies allowed having necessary flexibility to understand women's perception on the issues, which are generally not discussed. Though during the focus group discussions and in-depth interviews women shared their views on several issues, the present paper is concentrated on certain issues as under:

Family Planning: Contraception and Permanent Methods

Under the Rural Women Study all the three age groups, i.e., adolescent (11–15 years), young adults (16–35 years) and older adults (36–45 years) had shared their views and experiences about the contraception and permanent methods.

The adolescent girls had very little information about the various types of contraceptives. The information they had was inadequate and they were also wrongly informed.

The young adult is the group of women who are having immediate need of contraception. The women had information about various types of contraceptives. But, almost all of them reported to have sterilization as a method of family planning. Very few women reported using the contraceptives effectively. Two reasons could be seen behind this. One is that most of the women discontinued the use of contraceptives after having the initial negative experiences, which were not expected by them. The second reason is that they were not informed about the side effects of particular methods and the other options available, and were persuaded to go for permanent methods like tubectomy.

The women who had tried oral pills had many complaints like excessive discharge, early periods, burning in stomach, giddiness, increase in the body heat, etc. They also believed that the use of pills creates cancer. Thus, they were not informed about the possible side effects of the oral pills. The women also told that the health staff did not examine them before starting the pills. Besides, they were wrongly informed about the usage of the pills. For example, the health staff told a woman that whenever she would have sexual intercourse she should take the pill. Thus, the women who adopted to have oral contraception had to suffer many difficulties, as they were not informed properly. Improper use has led to pregnancies and conflicts in the couples. The women were asked to take pills, as there were targets to be achieved by the health staff.

The women were not properly informed as well about the Copper–T (Cu–T), its efficacy and side effects etc. The women who had used Cu-T also had many complaints like excessive discharge, stomach ache, pricking of Cu-T, weakness, etc. They were asked to use Cu-T only when they are likely to conceive a female child. Besides, if the female foetus was aborted, they were advised to use the Cu-T till the male child was conceived. This kind of perception was very confusing and made it clear that the women are wrongly informed.

Thus, the women were forced to use contraceptives without giving detailed information about their side effects, etc. Incorrect information also deprived the women from the expected results from the contraceptives. Further, the use of contraceptives was suggested to have male foetuses, thus the contraceptives were linked to prevent the birth of female babies. Under this study, not a single woman reported about condom use by her husband.

Under the Social RCH Study also, both the men and the women have reported their experiences about contraceptives. Though the women had information about the use of the oral pills, the source of knowledge was the media, particularly television. Though there is wide publicity about the oral pills through media, no information is provided about its usage and side effects. The women used the pills without proper information and medical advice and finally they had negative experiences and stopped using them. Though very few women opted for Cu-T, they were not provided timely and quality services. In spot observations it was found that the women who had come for Cu-T insertion were sent back for several reasons like non-availability of staff, sterilized instruments etc. Thus, such factors de-motivated the women to use such methods of spacing. The men said that they do not like to use condoms. Though the women had knowledge that the use of condom by men would protect them from STIs and AIDS, they could not insist their husbands to do so, because of violent clashes between them. In fact, the use of condom should be popularized among the men. But it is observed that only women are asked to convince their husbands to use condoms. The health staff never focuses on educating the men for condom use.

Permanent Methods of Family Planning

Under the Rural Women Study no women reported vasectomy as the method of family planning. Very few old adult women reported that their husbands had vasectomy when there was severe drought and the money was offered as an incentive for having it. The term 'kutumb niyojanache operation' was linked only with tubectomy. Though the women are expected to opt for permanent method like tubectomy, they cannot decide when to have it and after how many children. One woman rightly expressed: "Operation karayache ki nahi he gharchanchya vicharavar avalumbun" (Whether to have operation or not depends on husband's wish).

When the women have only daughters, they cannot undergo operation even if they are not willing to have more pregnancies. While some women reported that they have to opt for re-canalization if the husband decides to have more sons. Though the women were aware that they might face health problems like backache, disturbances in menstruation cycle, white discharge and weakness, they had to accept the operations as the men wanted them to have it. The women under the Social RCH Study also reported similar complaints. They also did not report the vasectomy as a family planning method. Under both the studies there were very strong reactions regarding the attitudes of the health staff towards women and the tubectomies. The women under both studies reported that they are paid more attention by the health staff if they are 'operation cases'. Under the Rural Women Study it was reported that the ANM does not provide the immunization and other services to the women who are not 'possible cases'. They are not even attended for deliveries etc. But, the staff approach them later and insist that they should have tubectomy. If they take help of any other staff, the health staff rudely treat them and do not provide other services like immunization to their children, advice about the spacing methods etc. Their other health complaints are totally neglected.

Under the Social RCH Study also, the similar apathy on the part of health staff was noticed. The spot observations showed that the health staff insist on operations and do not provide information about other spacing methods or vasectomy. On scrutiny the three months' record showed that there was only one vasectomy against 101 tubectomies.

Further, it was observed that the health staff has very indifferent attitude towards the women whose tubectomy fails and they come for re-operation. It was found that such women had to offer bribes to the medical officers and to get re-operated. The whole health system, whether rural or urban, does not take any responsibility for failure of these cases. The women have to face another pregnancies, and are indebted either in going to private services or paying bribes to the medical officers at government hospitals. It also invites the health risks as the pregnancy advances during the process of negotiating with the medical officers for termination of pregnancy and tubectomy. This process forces the women to go to private hospitals as the pregnancy advances and it becomes impossible to have termination of pregnancy at the government hospitals.

The data on the medical termination of pregnancy (MTP) also shows that the women are forced to opt for MTP along with the tubectomy. There were 52 MTPs during the period of three months, of which 24 had MTP with tubectomy, while 20 had Cu-T after the MTP and only eight women had simply MTP. It was reported that there are oral guidelines given by the government that as far as possible only MTP should not be allowed and it should be followed by tubectomy. Thus, the women who want to have MTP in case of unintended pregnancy are forced to have tubectomies also and thus they are not able to have control on their fertility by using other spacing methods.

Thus, on the whole, these two studies about contraception and family planning show that there is strong gender bias and the women are targeted for family planning. The policy planners and programme implementers have further strengthened the society's attitude that "it is women's domain or their issue". Thus, the women are solely held responsible for controlling the population and are treated as the objects for family planning targets. The gender bias also reflects through various ways the women are not given the choice to control their fertility by spacing methods. It is so strong that there is little or no advocacy for vasectomies. It is interesting to note that the formats of the reports of the RCH programme do not have even the column to report the vasectomies, and there is reporting about the tubectomies only. The incentives and concessions in user fees for women who undergo tubectomies also further show the gender bias.

Thus, statistical data, spot observations and discussions with the health staff, and the careful analysis of the guidelines/policy issued by the government, corroborate the women's perception that there is strong gender bias and they are targeted for family planning. There seems to be blindfold on the fact that the men have the equal role in controlling the population. Thus, women's very first reproductive health right to have control on their own bodies and enjoy the sexual life without fears is grossly violated. They have fears of unintended pregnancies, sexually transmitted infections and HIV/AIDS and have become unnecessary victims of these.

Health Seeking Behaviour and Women

The above discussion on the family planning shows that in India all health services are geared towards the population control, considering women as targets. It is necessary to understand whether the women's health can be limited to their childbearing role only? Under the Rural Women Study, the women had listed 163 general health problems, while women-specific health problems listed by different groups were: adolescents–86, young adults–62, and old adults–53. Under the Social RCH Study the women have reported more health complaints than the men. The women in the childbearing age and the women at menopause have reported highest number of health complaints, i.e., 29 and 36 respectively.

Figure 1

Health Seeking Pattern in Women-Specific Illnesses

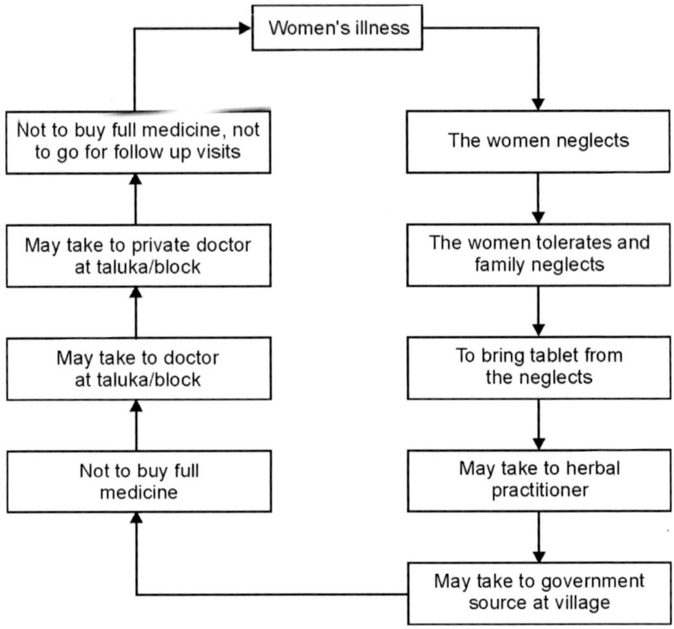

Several studies conducted in different parts of India have revealed that there is large-scale morbidity among women due to reproductive health problems. Likewise, both the studies discussed above have also shown that the women face many difficulties in seeking treatment for their health problems. The Rural Women Study has revealed a definite pattern for health seeking in case of rural women's illnesses as depicted in Figure 1. There are few variations with different illnesses. But it does not mean that with growing age, women have gained more access to health seeking. The initial reaction of the women themselves towards the illness is that of negligence. In case of women the treatment effort starts from less expensive source. Majority of the women do not complete the treatment, as the prescribed medicines are not brought fully, follow-up visits are not made and referrals to other services are not done. In other words, treatment is not completed, relief is temporary and there is relapse of the illness. The incomplete treatment leads to more complications and makes it more expensive. As it becomes more expensive the possibility of treating the illness completely reduces. The husband or the 'Malak' (owner) is the sole decision-maker about the wife's treatment. This decision-making is affected by the husband's knowledge about the illness, availability of time, money and person to accompany the woman. The women have to face this discrimination even though they are equal wage earners in the family. Though the treatment effort starts from less expensive source, the women do not find the government sources useful, as it does not provide services for most of the reproductive health illnesses. The present health services cater women only during pregnancy. Further, the health staff have gender and caste bias which affects women's health seeking behaviour. Though the experiences with the private doctors were better, in case of abortions there is space for doubt that the private practitioners motivate the women and the families to go for sex determination.

The Social RCH Study has also shown that though the poor women consider government hospitals as the cheapest source of treatment, the services are very inadequate to cater to reproductive health needs of the women. Both these studies and studies conducted in other parts of India have revealed that there is wide prevalence of health complaints like painful menstruation, heavy discharge, white discharge, uterus prolapse, STIs, anaemia etc. But, as the health staff have the pressure of completing targets of tubectomies, the women with other health complaints are perceived as the 'extra work'. During the spot observations, it was found that the women with complaints like excessive discharge were sent back when there were holidays for consecutive two-three days. The women with complaints like white discharge were labelled as the women who had no *akkal* (knowledge) and were sent back without any guidance and treatment. It was expected that the complaint of white discharge should be accepted as normal. But, the discussion with the women reveals that the women have observed certain signs and symptoms when they would recognize that it was not normal.

The health staff reflected strong gender and caste bias. The women from the so-called lower communities were not physically checked. The illiterate and very poor women were greeted with the harsh language and they were also asked to keep some distance from the doctor.

The practices of taking bribes and corruption further kept the women away from the treatment or forced to discontinue.

Both the studies revealed that there is no support system in case of women's long-term illness. When the complications increase, treating the women's illness becomes more difficult. Long-term illness may result in deserting the women. When the husband's family neglects the illness, the only support is the natal family, but due to poor economic situation, most of the women do not get this. Many women reported that the illnesses like red or white discharge, backache, anaemia, prolapsed uterus, STIs etc. were untreated. The women become the silent sufferers as most of the illnesses are not visible unless they themselves share it and family, especially the husband, understands its severity. Many women were found to be in morbidity due to red/white discharge for more than 7–10 years and suffering due to other complaints like anaemia also.

The present studies and the other studies like that conducted in rural Karnataka reported untreated morbidity as 44–57 per cent (Bhatia and Cleland, 1995). Similarly, 92 per cent tribal women in Maharashtra (Bang et al., 1989) had not sought any treatment for gynecological morbidity.

The present Reproductive and Child Health Programme is mostly preventive in nature. It also focuses more on the maternal health and neglected several other reproductive health complaints. The present health services cannot provide treatment to several complaints reported by the women. This nature of government services has also opened the alternative of private services. But women's access to private curative health services becomes difficult when it comes to spending more money.

Further, the globalization has impacted the health care significantly. Under the globalization and privatization the state investment in health sector is declining, the drug prices are rapidly increasing, which is resulting in reduced access of poor to private services (Duggal, 2001). At the global level the World Bank is propagating selective care for targeted populations and the ailments like AIDS are receiving more support (Duggal, 2001). With such policies the women's health problems, besides maternal health and other general health complaints, are likely to receive no attention.

The deep-rooted gender bias in child socialization develops in the women themselves the attitude of negligence towards their ill-health. Besides the neglect on the part of family, the government programmes are also insensitive to their health needs. Though there is high prevalence of women's health programmes, they remain in morbidity, which affects their productivity.

The CEDAW has affirmed that the access to the health care, including reproductive health, is a basic right of women. It further states that the interventions should aim at both the prevention and treatment of diseases and conditions affecting women. It continues to say that the state should ensure universal access for all women to a full range of high quality and affordable health care, including sexual and RCH services.

The above discussion based on field level data from poor rural and urban women makes it clear that the women's right to access the health services is grossly violated. Further, the right to have need-based services is totally neglected and the women are targeted for population control only.

Access to Food and Women's Health

Under the Rural Women Study, while talking about various illnesses and reasons behind them, women referred several times to food in different contexts. The women's reactions show that the whole issue of food for women had socio-cultural context. The issue of women and food could be discussed from four different angles as depicted in the Figure 2.

Lack of Food

Most of the women reported that they drink excessive tea and it leads to several health complaints. When the issue was further probed in details, it was revealed that it relates to lack of food. The following statement by one of the women is indicative of the women's access to food: "In some families the situation is critical, food is not available, in these families, getting food for 2–3 days is not possible, then women in these families manage the days with tea".

Figure 2

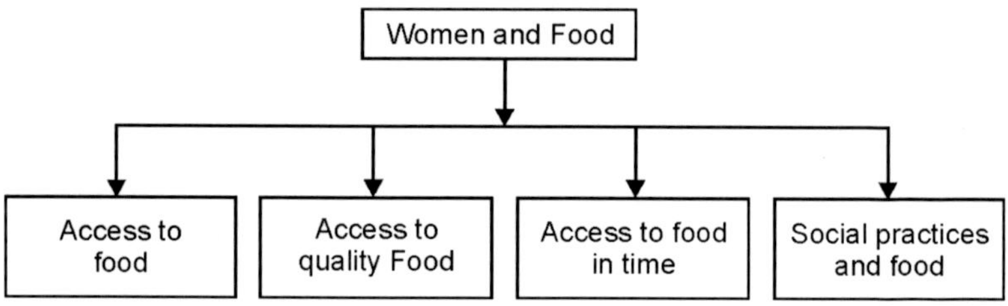

It is important to recall that the study was conducted in the drought-prone region and majority of the women came from economically poor families. It is possible that many women may not share this as it affects the prestige of the family. The lack of food may vary according to seasons, as in rural areas the work is not available in certain seasons. Eating stale food was one of the reasons reported for stomach ache. The women reacted that they could not afford to waste food and had to eat stale food. It would be interested to note that the women who waste food are criticized in the community for not having good habits. Almost all women under the study reported the complaint of anaemia or weakness, and majority of them related weakness to food. The women's access to food in the drought-prone area is difficult, as the family does not earn to buy enough food for its members and in the scarcity situation the women's access to food becomes difficult. Thus, the women's access to food itself is an issue of great concern.

Access to Quality Food

Weakness and backache were the most prevalent complaints in all the three age-group women. The reason provided for these complaints was that the women do not get quality food. The young adult and older adult women felt that on certain occasions like childbirth or after family planning operation they need quality food. But, they do not get such food, mainly due to poor economic situation. While most of the younger adult women felt that if they could get quality food, they will not fall ill. The women further defined the 'quality food' as raw vegetables like tomatoes, carrots, leafy vegetables, sprouted pluses, fruits, ghee (clarified butter), wheat chappati, eggs etc. The women reported eating leafy vegetables, salads, fruits as home remedies for weakness, but were also quite aware that they cannot afford to buy them. They said that they have to give preference to the children.

The women also believed that hybrid varieties of food grains and vegetables do not give enough 'shakti' as it is not nutritious.

Thus women's access to quality food is denied due to poor economic situation of the family. When a family is unable to buy enough quantities of required food the women's access to quality food becomes more difficult as the children and men get priority. This leads to weakness, which in turn may give rise to several other health problems. The latest data by National Family Health Survey 2 (2000) also has revealed that 51.8 per cent of women are anaemic.

Access to Food in Time

Besides lack of food and access to quality food, the women also stated not to have food in time as a reason for the health ailments. The rural women are overburdened with work and have to look after both farm and house. There is also sexual division of labour in the household as well as on the farm. Women are pressurized to complete the work in time. Incomplete work invites violence by the in-laws and the husband. This attitude denies their access to food in time. Besides, the rural women are also expected to eat after the elders in the family and the husband. The women who do not follow it are considered to be 'bad women'. Thus excessive pressure of work and certain social taboos deny women's access to food in time.

Social Practices and Women's Food Security

One of the frequently provided reasons for anaemia was "not to have food for two-three days". Further probing the issue revealed many facts. It was found that majority of women from all the three age-groups observe several fasts. The estimations for the year showed that on an average a woman keeps usual fasts for 72–75 days, in addition to several special fasts in a year. Though there is some special food, which is prescribed for the fast days, but buying or eating it is out of their economic capacities.

It should be noted that as most of the women under the study were from economically poor families, observing religious fasts might be giving the socially acceptable label for the lack of food security in the household, especially for the women. This study has given some evidence about the lack of food security to women in the drought-prone and backward region.

Thus, rural women's access to food is difficult. When the families do not have sufficient incomes, the women's access to food is denied, let alone leave the access to quality food. Then, the gender bias in the division of work also makes it difficult for women to get food in time. The families and society try to label the food insecurity for women by religious way. Food insecurity makes the women anaemic and lack of enough quantity and quality food keeps them in lifetime morbidity as their access to food is at stake at all stages of their life cycle.

Women's nutritional status is one of the major indicators of health and development as well. Under the CEDAW it is expected that the state would intervene in both the prevention and treatment of diseases and conditions affecting the women. The food is essential for good health, and when the basic food security is not ensured, the women become the victims of starvation in a gender bias society. Thus, the issue of food insecurity for the women should be given a prime focus in development plans along with providing services to deal with the anaemia and other health problems.

Women's Empowerment for Health: TISSRC Experience

The above discussion has shared the women's perceptions about gender bias and how their reproductive rights are violated. The scenario of women's health would not be positive unless their status in the society is improved.

Dixson (1978) has defined women's status as "the degree of women's access to (and control over) material resources (including food, income, land and other forms of wealth) and to social resources (knowledge, power and prestige) within the family, in the community and in the society at large". The discrimination and poor access to resources affect their health. To eliminate the discrimination and gender bias the women need to be empowered about their own health needs.

As there are cultural, social, religious and economic disparities in the Indian society, the area need-based approach for women's empowerment is required. It is necessary to have demonstration of models, which would show some results regarding women's empowerment. TISSRC, through its project "Health Resource Centre", has developed some modules for women's empowerment. The next part of this paper presents one module, which dealt with the issue of difficulties in health seeking and the domestic violence. This has demonstrated that if the need-based modules of women's empowerment are introduced, the women can improve their own situation.

The findings of the Rural Women Study were shared with the communities from the villages covered under the study. The concept of Health Resource Centre (HRC) was evolved to keep people well-informed and develop their skills to deal various issues related to health and development (see Figure 3). The HRC had focused on organizing the people for their health issues, providing research and database needs for the same and to build up the capacity of the people, especially women. The HRC's approach is to create the animators/resource persons in the community itself, who would take a leadership role in organizing the people for their health problems. To achieve this, the core group of women was developed through the conscious process of identifying the women with the leadership qualities. Thus, the care was taken to select women from each community pocket. It also helped to include the key women like women members in PRIs, dais, anganwadi workers, health staff etc. Thus, a group of 30–35 women came out. There was series of discussions with this group. Simultaneously, the Self-Help Groups (SHGs) were found as effective platform to have continuous dialogue with women on a large scale. The women realized that creating a new set up of services would be difficult. The reflections in the discussions made it clear that the women's health seeking could be improved by providing information to women themselves and by their participation in community monitoring of various government services at village. The services like health sub-centre, anganwadi, school, ration shop (distribution centre under Public Distribution System) etc. were mainly focused. The women also felt necessary to understand Gram Panchayat as it plays key role in decision-making at village level.

Figure 3

Concept of Health Resource Centre

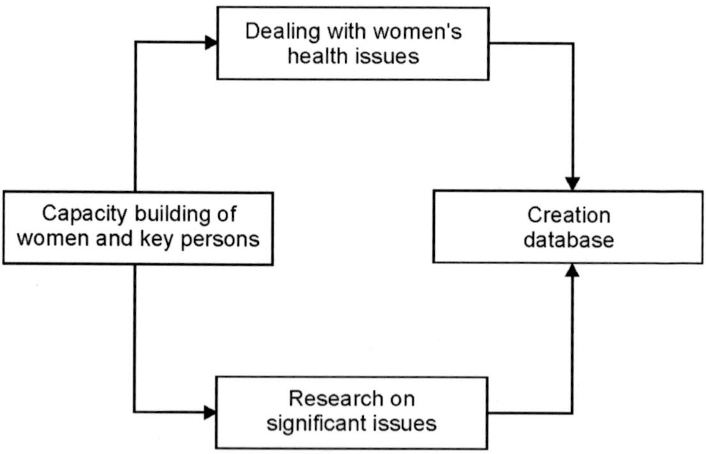

The domestic violence was one of the major problems reported by the women. Hence, the effort was also made to inform them about the available support systems. The core group was motivated to give feedback to men in the villages about the information and other inputs they were receiving; there was also constant dialogue with the men about the process followed with the core group, which helped to evolve their support.

After the group formation process the capacity building training module was conducted. This module included understanding of the factors affecting the health, understanding the health services, exposure to health/support services, and understanding the role of facilitators in the process. Figure 4 shows components of the training. Different methodology was adopted. It included one-day classroom session, followed by the field visit to the related services available in the community. The classroom session focused on understanding the realities about their own village and having dialogue with the concerned government staff. The effort was to have discussion on various factors, which affected the health seeking. These sessions were very participatory in nature considering the lower literacy level of the women.

Figure 4

Health Seeking and Dealing with Violence Module

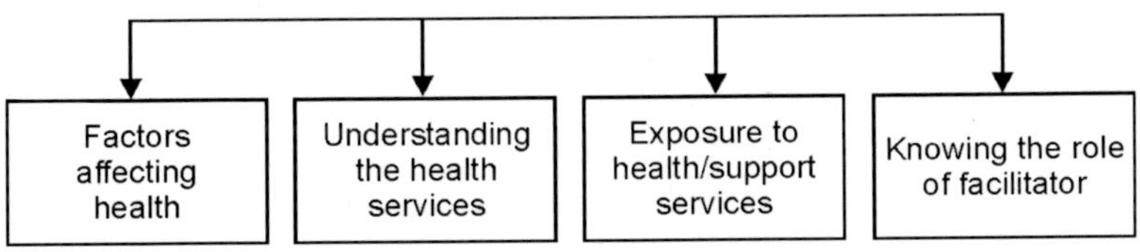

The visits included sub-centre at village, anganwadi (a village-level centre under Integrated Child Development Scheme for children, pregnant and lactating mothers), Gram Panchayat, Rural Hospital at taluka headquarters and the Civil Hospital at the district headquarters. The visits were also made to Police Station, Mahila Takrar Nivaran Kendra and two NGOs working on violence and women's health issues. The visits also included Panchayat Samiti (Block Development Office), Lead Bank, District Industrial Centre and Post office. The group also visited TISSRC Office to understand its role in facilitating the HRC and there were also demonstrations about the use of computers, e-mails, fax, telephone etc. to understand the role of information technology in facilitating the health seeking.

Outcome of the Empowerment Module

The results were evident during the process of the training itself. Some changes were quantitative while majority changes were qualitative in nature. To begin with the women took up the issue of defunct health services. The series of discussions through SHGs and the signature campaign was taken up. The group of women delegates also had discussion with the district health authority. This resulted in revitalization of the sub-centre. The OPD was started and it led to 15 patients per day from no patients. The ANM was closely monitored for providing the services like weighing, Hb checking under antenatal care etc. The ANM and MPW (health staff at the sub-centre level) also started residing in the village.

The awareness about the available services increased. Almost all births were attended by the ANM. The knowledge about the available services was reflected through using government facilities like incubators for underweight babies etc.

The increased contact with the ANM through SHGs' meetings and formation of Health Committee helped develop the positive relationship with the health staff.

The session on "what is violence" followed by the visits to support systems motivated the women to become more vocal about the violence they faced. The self-reporting of the violence increased. The core group women intervened, referred and followed up nearly 25 cases. The guidance was provided to them whenever required and counselling was given by the trained social workers. Overall, the awareness about the support systems available within the close periphery was increased. This was reflected through the discussions, dealing with the cases etc.

As the Gram Panchayat is known to be a male-dominated place, most of the women never had visited it or had discussion with the male members of the panchayat. As the result of the empowerment module, the women started attending the Gram Sabhas (village meetings for key decisions under the Gram

Panchayat Act). The women also started taking interest in monitoring various development schemes being implemented by the Gram Panchayat.

The women's overall participation in the development programme increased. The women collected *Lokwata*, i.e., people's contribution for school building compound as a result of dialogue with the school teachers during the training. The *Mata Bal Sangh* also became active. The women's participation in the awareness generation programme through schools was also evident.

This module established the fact that the area and need-based approach towards women's empowerment is essential and conscious efforts could bring the changes in women's capacities in dealing with their health issues.

Conclusions

The present paper, based on the two qualitative studies, has clearly shown that Indian women are the victims of gender bias. This gender bias is strongly reflected in rural women and poor urban women. The reproductive health rights of these women are violated in various ways. The women are targeted for population control. They are considered as 'objects' and not 'subjects' for change. They are denied their basic reproductive health right of having control over own bodies. The complete denial of the men's role in population growth clearly reflects the gender bias not only of the society but the policy planners as well.

Further, insensitive health services to the health needs of the women continue to violate their reproductive health rights. They are wrongly informed about contraception and are left to face the ill, effects. The present health services fail to fulfil the health needs of the women. The health services perceive the women as only producers of the children and forget them as individuals.

The health cannot be considered in separation but correlates with the development of the weaker sections of society. Various development indicators relate to the health status of various weaker sections, especially the women and the children, in any given society. The CEDAW document has rightly stated that there should not be treatment only of diseases but the conditions affecting the women. The issues like food security for the women, violence against women and education are still not addressed, even partially too.

There is violation of basic reproductive health rights and women's access to quality and need-based health services is denied, hence it should become the issue of women's empowerment. But, the empowerment is a process and it cannot be achieved unless consciously thought of. The health policy has to be shifted from the service orientation and focus on how to empower the women for their own health. Considering the vast cultural differences and needs of Indian women grassroots demonstrations of empowerment modules are required. The TISSRC has successfully demonstrated one of such modules of empowering the women for their own health with the involvement of the present health staff. It is required that such successful strategies should be integrated into policy to protect women's reproductive health rights.

References

Arora, Dolly. 1999. 'Structural Adjustment Programme and Gender Concerns in India', *Journal of Contemporary Asia,* Vol. 29, No. 3.

Bang, R.A., Bang A.T. et. al. 1989. 'High Prevalence of Gynecological Diseases in Rural Indian Women', *The Lancet,* January, 14.

Batliwala, Shrilatha. 1993. 'Empowerment of Women in South Asia: Concepts and Practices', FFHC, FAO, New Delhi.

Bhasin, Kamala. 1993. *What is Patriarchy?*. New Delhi: Kali for Women.

Bhatia, J. and Cleland J. 1996. 'Obstetric Morbidity in South India: Results from Community Survey', *Social Sciences Medicine* I.

Bandewar, S. and Saha, S. 2000. 'Studies in Reproductive Health Services in India'. (1990–99) CEHAT.

CHETANA. 1996. Convention on the Elimination of all Forms of Discrimination Against Women (CEDAW) – An Alternative Report By NGOs – Article 12, Health Care Services (Summary). Ahmedabad.

Datar, Chhaya (ed.). 1993. *The Struggle Against Violence.* Kolkata: Stree.

Davar, B. 1999. *Mental Health of Indian Women: A Feminist Agenda.* New Delhi: Sage Publications.

Duggal R. 2001. 'Globalization and Health Sector Reforms in India'. CEHAT Mumbai.

George, A. et. al. 1994. 'Women's Reproductive Health and Sexuality – An Annotated Bibliography', Dept. of Health Services Studies, Tata Institute of Social Sciences, Bombay.

Gopalan, S. and Shiva, M. 2000. 'National Profile on Women, Health and Development – Country Profile – India', Voluntary Health Association of India, World Health Organization.

Human Development Report Maharashtra – 2002.

Jandhyal, Kameshwari. 1997. 'Women and Development: Some Observations From the Field'. *In* Haleh Afshar and Fatima Ali (eds.) *Empowering Women for Development: Experiences from some Third World Countries,* Hyderabad: Booklink Corporation. pp. 88–102.

Jane, Stein. 1997. *Empowerment and Women's Health: Theory, Methods and Practice.* London & New Jersey: Zed Books.

Jo, Rowlands. 1997. 'What is Empowerment?'. *In* Haleh Afshar and Fatima Ali (eds.) *Empowering Women for Development: Experiences from Some Third World Countries,* Hyderabad: Booklink Corporation.

Kishwar, Madhu. 1988. 'Nature of Women's Mobilization in Rural India-An Exploratory Essay', *Economic and Political Weekly,* December 24–31. pp. 2754–2763.

Kulkarni, Anjali. 1999. 'Women's Access to Natural Resources: The Need of Advocacy for Grassroots Demonstrations'. A paper presented at 8th National Conference by IAWS on Survival and Sovereignty: Challenge to Women's Studies, May, Pune.

—. 1999. 'Access to Natural Resources and Women's Empowerment', *Ashwattha* Yashada, Pune, Vol. 2 No. 2, April–June.

—. 1999. 'Perspective paper on Women's Health in Rural Maharashtra' unpublished. A paper written for Rural Campus, Tata Institute of Social Sciences, Tuljapur, Dist. Osmanabad.

—. 2002. 'Anemia: A Life-Long Problem of Indian Rural Women'. A paper presented at 10th National Conference of IAWS Sustaining Democracy: Challenges in the New Millennium 17–20th October, Bhubaneswar.

—. 2002. 'Women's Health and Globalization'. A paper presented at Regional Conference on Women's Development and Challenges of Globalization: Gender Sensitivity in Teaching at Undergraduate Level at Tuljapur, Dist. Osmanabad, January.

Lingam, L. (ed.). *Understanding Women's Health Issues: A Reader*. New Delhi: Kali for Women.

Lucia Hanmer. 1994. 'Equity and Gender Issues in Health Care Provision: The World Bank Development Report and its Implications for Health Service Recipients'. Working Paper Series No. 172, Institute of Social Studies, The Hague , The Netherlands.

Madhurima. 1996. *Violence Against Women: Dynamics at Conjugal Relations,* New Delhi: Gyan Publishing House.

Mary, E. John. 1996. 'Gender and Development in India, 1970s –1990s: Some Reflections on the Constitutive Role of Contexts', *Economic and Political Weekly,* November 23. pp. 3071–3077.

Mathur, I. and Sharma S. 1995. *"Health Hazards, Gender and Society".* Jaipur: Rawat Publications.

National Family Health Survey NFHS–2: Maharashtra (2000), International Institute of Population Sciences, Mumbai.

National Family Health Survey NFHS–2: India Key Findings (2000), International Institute of Population Sciences, Mumbai.

Patricia, Smith. 1993. *On Equality: Justice, Discrimination and Equal Treatment. Feminist Jurisprudence,* Oxford University Press.

Pillai, Jaya K. 1995. *Women and Empowerment,* New Delhi: Gyan Publishing House.

Quadeer I. and Sen K. 2001. *Public Health and the Poverty Reforms: The South Asian Predicament,* New Delhi: Sage Publications.

Ralhan, O.P. (ed.). 1995. *Indian Women Through Ages,* Vol. 4 *Women and Modernity,* New Delhi: Anmol Publications Pvt. Ltd.

Saskia, Weiringa. 1994. 'Women's Interests and Empowerment: Gender Planning Reconsidered', *Development and Change,* ISS, The Hague, Vol. 25, No. 4, pp. 829–849.

Sathe, S.P. (undated). 'Women, Development and Gender Justice'. Source IALS, Pune.

Sharma, O.P. 2000. *Rural Health and Medical Care in India,* New Delhi: Manak Publications Pvt. Ltd.

8

Undertrial Women Prisoners and Human Rights

SMRITI BHOSLE

Human rights have evolved out of mankind's increasing demands for a life in which the inherent dignity and worth of each human being is respected and protected. It is now expected that there are certain rights which are inevitable for the dignified existence of a human being. That a dignity of a human being should be respected seems to be the basic to all such rights. Human dignity is a core value of Indian Constitution and the courts, while interpreting Article 21, have demonstrated that every person is entitled to a quality life, consistent with his human personality.

The right to life and liberty guaranteed in the Constitution of India is the primary source of criminal law. This right is then translated into Indian Penal Code, Criminal Procedure Code and Evidence Act and also in local and special laws. The Directive Principles of State Policy set down the responsibility of the state to provide for free legal aid, where required (for reasons of economic or other disabilities). This is to ensure equal justice for all citizens and to further the guarantee of equality before the law, as provided in Article 14 of the Constitution.

Articles 3 and 9 of the Universal Declaration of Human Rights also provide for the right to life, liberty and security and protection from arbitrary arrests, detention or exile. The Supreme Court has also emphasized that even the convicts have right to dignity and whatever liberty they are left cannot be taken away arbitrarily. Article 5 of the Universal Declaration of Human Rights 1948 provides that "no one shall be subjected to torture or to cruel inhuman or degrading treatment or punishment".

The National Expert Committee on Women Prisoners (1987) with Justice Krishna Iyer as its chairman stated after visiting many women prisons that prisoners and the prison staff suffer from what was called by the Supreme Court "the pathology of misinformation or ignorance about rights and limitations". This often leads to callous disregard of human rights. Similarly, courts also fail to show proper awareness of women forming a special category, especially those with minor children or bread-earning responsibilities in cases of female-headed households.

It is disturbing to note that there is prolonged imprisonment of undertrial women who constitute more than 70 per cent of female jail population of the country. There are undertrial women languishing for 4–5 years in jails for offences for which the sentence would have been far less if they had been convicted. Many women prisoners continue in jails for long periods as they are unable to defend themselves and ignorant of the ways and means of securing legal help and thus totally at the mercy of the jail officers, who often fail to show any understanding of their problems.

In our country, rights of prisoner is hardly a matter of concern. The fact that prisoner is also a human being is often forgotten by us and lost of our sight. One of the fundamental reasons behind this is our primitive notion about the punishment. All over the world the notion about punishment is being converted to reformative from retributive framework but in our country the concept regarding punishment is still retributive in its nature. We do have a good number of statutes, rules, regulations and Acts regarding the treatment of prisoners, but those are not being fairly prosecuted. In this context, our penal policy and prison system lag behind not only civilized standard but also UN standard.

Criminal Justice System

The criminal justice system involves criminal prevention, detection, apprehension, adjudication and punishment. It includes all those agencies such as the police, correctional institutes, courts and legislatures that are responsible for enforcing criminal laws.

The criminal justice system may be viewed under the following sub-heads:

The Police System

Modern police system in India was established by the colonial government. The Indian Police Act, 1861 provided for a uniform system of police force in India. The powers and functions are derived from this statute. Besides power of arrest, search, seizure and investigation of offences have been conferred on the police by the Code of Criminal Procedure. The Criminal Procedure Code, 1898, which had undergone minor changes from time to time, was later repealed and replaced by the Code of Criminal Procedure, 1973.

Alleged Offence

The criminal justice process, in the case of a cognizable offence, may be set into motion either on the complaint of an aggrieved individual, or citizen (as witness), or by the police itself on receipt of information. In the case of non-cognizable offences, which are generally viewed as disputes of a civil nature (for instance, family or neighbourhood quarrels), the police cannot act unless a formal accusation has been lodged in the police station.

In short, offences are divided under the Criminal Procedure Code into two categories: cognizable and non-cognizable. A cognizable offence is one for which any police officer may arrest without a warrant. When he does not have that power under the law, the offence is non-cognizable.

Arrest

Arrest is the act of taking a person into custody in order to make a criminal charge against the person. The arrested person must be informed of the ground of his arrest, his right to bail and to engage a counsel/lawyer. But some officers are not conscious of their duty and they do not inform the accused of the grounds of his/her arrest. They usually assume that the accused is aware of such rights.

A person arrested without a warrant cannot be detained for more than 24 hours from the time of his arrest exclusive of travelling time from the police station to the court. Usually investigation cannot be completed within 24 hours, so the magistrate may authorize detention of the accused in police custody for not more than 15 days. This is known as remand.

Police Custody

When the police decide to take a suspect into custody to pursue further inquiry or prevent the commission of further violation, it is known as arrest or police custody. This can be done under judicial sanction with warrant or without warrant.

The police may identify possible suspects on the basis of evidence or suspicion. In order to pursue the inquiry or to prevent the commission for further violation, the police may decide to take a suspect into custody (that is arrest him or her). Ordinarily judicial sanction is required for an arrest, in the form of a warrant. However, arrest without warrant is also permissible in certain cases. This is rationalized on the grounds that quick action is necessary to prevent a suspect from escaping, tampering with evidence, or committing another offence.

Police custody is not free from fear and anxiety. Offenders always remain in constant fear of possible torture and abuse. The first offenders also face mental and emotional shock and damage to their reputation. The offenders during police custody have to face accommodation, diet and other difficulties.

The offender's first encounter with the criminal justice process is in a police lock-up where he is temporarily confined before being produced before a magistrate or on remand of police custody.

Once a person is arrested, he/she is kept in police custody, so as to be available to the police for its investigation. If the offence is bailable, the suspect can make arrangements for bail through persons related or otherwise known, or lawyers. But if the offence is non-bailable and bail is rejected by the court, or cannot be arranged for by the prisoner, the latter continues to remain in custody (but may ask for a transfer to prison as an undertrial).

Police Investigation

Under Chapter XII of the Criminal Procedure Code, the police has a statutory right to carry on investigation. Investigation generally through interviews and interrogation is most important in criminal trial. The scientific investigation can help in arriving at correct conclusions. Investigation of an offence is the field exclusively of the police department. The police have the bounden duty to investigate and it is their duty to collect the evidence for the purpose of providing the evidence.

Filing the Chargesheet

Information relating to the commission of a cognizable offence which is given orally must be written down by a police officer. This is known as the First Information Report (FIR) and it must be signed by the informant and must be entered in a prescribed book by the officer. When a police officer has completed investigation, he must make an official report to the magistrate. The completed report is known as chargesheet. A chargesheet consists of the police reports, the FIR and all documents relating to the offences and confessions and statements of witnesses, etc. A copy of the chargesheet is also given to the accused. Once the chargesheet is submitted, the power of the police to investigate comes to an end. The police cannot now interfere with the investigation of the magistrate court. But, according to a new provision in the Criminal Procedure Code, i.e., Section 173(8), even after submission of the chargesheet, a police officer may make further investigation in respect of an offence and send to the magistrate any further reports regarding any additional evidence obtained by him.

Prosecution

This process starts when the state begins the formal process of inquiry and detection of crime in a criminal case. Action is taken by a prosecuting attorney, a government official, whose duty is to initiate and maintain criminal proceedings on behalf of the government against persons accused of committing crimes.

Prison Custody

When the police no longer require the individual for the purposes of investigation, he/she is given prison custody.

As mentioned earlier, if a prisoner in police custody is not released on bail, he or she may request a transfer to prison custody. This may occur even otherwise, when the police no longer require the individual for the purposes of investigation. While in prison, the undertrial continues to be remanded and produced in court on the next date given. This process of giving remand may go on for weeks or months before the hearing actually starts.

Detention

It is holding up in prison between arrest and trial, either because the judge has refused bail or the defendant cannot meet the requirements of bail. Generally, the purpose is to assure the presence of the accused at trial.

Trial

From now on, the role of the court begins. The criminal court is the core of the criminal justice process. It has the duty to supervise the work of the police, prosecutor and defence counsel and implement the laws. A trial is a court proceeding during which the judge listens to the evidence as presented by the defence and the prosecution, and determines whether the defendant or accused is guilty beyond a reasonable doubt or not. On completion of investigation, the police must file charges in court. The charge sheet becomes the basis of the trial.

A fair trial implies a speedy trial. However, there is no specific criterion of promptness. The Indian Constitution does not specifically guarantee to the accused the right to a speedy trial. But Article 21, along with Articles 14, 38, 39 and 39-A, makes it a necessary concomitant of social justice promised in the preamble.

Appeal

An accused may apply to a higher court for release on bail, or modification of bail conditions stipulated by the police or lower court. He or she may also appeal against the decision of the trial court. In the case of a death sentence, the final appeal for mercy lies with the President of India.

Bail

Bail implies money or property posted by the defendant after arrest and before trial to guarantee that he or she will appear for trial, sentencing or imprisonment. If the defendant does not appear, the money or property is forfeited to the state. Liberty is a most valuable right and when the accused applies for bail, he or she seeks this right from the court. In offences which are specified in the code as bailable, bail is a matter of right. And, if the offence is specified as non-bailable, bail is a matter of discretion. Bail may be granted by the court or by the officer-in-charge of a police station. If the person fails to appear in court on the given date or tampers with the evidence/witnesses, then, the bail order can be revoked and he or she will be arrested and imprisoned.

Police Escort

While in custody, a prisoner is taken from one place to another for various reasons, for instance, from lock-up to court or hospital and back. All these visits must necessarily be under police escort, even when the person is transferred to prison as an undertrial. Women constables are required to be present for escorting women prisoners to court.

Legal Aid

Legal aid is crucial for a suspect and each individual has the right to obtain it. The Supreme Court has even held that free legal services are the "constitutional right of every accused person who is unable to engage a lawyer and secure legal services on account of reasons such as poverty, indigence or incommunicable situation and the state is under a mandate to provide a lawyer to an accused person if the circumstances of the case and the needs of justice so require". It is also important to note here that legal aid is urgent for the suspect from the moment of detention, and not only during the trial.

In short, the complexities of substantive and procedural laws require a specialized mediator – lawyer. Menon has stated that "the legal process is quite cumbersome and presents a financial liability to the accused particularly when he is poor and illiterate".[1] If the right to counsel is essential to fair trial, it is important that the accused has the necessary means for his defence. Section 304 of the Criminal Procedure Code deals with legal aid to the accused at the expense of the state.

Legal Provisions for Women Prisoners

Specific legal and administrative provisions exist with respect to women suspects and prisoners. These provisions are intended to provide directions to the police, courts and prison authorities in the handling of women prisoners.

Prison Act, 1894

1. Section 24(3) provides that in the case of female prisoners, the search and examination (on admission) shall be carried out by the matron under the general or special orders of the Medical Officer.
2. Section 27(1) provides that in a prison inhabiting female as well as male prisoners, the females shall be imprisoned in separate buildings, or separate parts of the same building, in such manner as to prevent their seeing, or conversing or holding any intercourse with male prisoners.

3. Section 46 states that no female shall be liable to the imposition of any form of handcuffs or letters, or to whipping, as punishment for prison offences.

Criminal Manual Issued by the High Court of Bombay, 1960

Women accused of any offence, if arrested soon after childbirth, cannot be at once taken before thc magistrate as this may cause personal suffering and risk to health. They should not ordinarily, be removed until they are in a proper condition to travel. In such cases, sanction must be obtained by the police from the nearest magistrate for their detention at their homes, or in the dispensary beyond a period of 24 hours allowed by Section 61 of the Criminal Procedure Code.

Criminal Procedure Code, 1973

1. Sections 51(2) and 100(3) make it obligatory that a woman should be searched by woman, and with strict regard to decency.
2. Section 160(1) prohibits the police from requiring any woman to appear at any place other than the place of her residence for the purpose of examination by police.
3. Section 53(2) states that the medical examination of a female accused should be conducted only by or under the supervision of a woman medical practitioner.
4. Section 437 provides that in the case of a non-bailable offence, a court (not being the sessions or high court) may direct a woman accused to be released on bail.
5. Section 360(1) provides that a woman of any age, if convicted of an offence (not punishable with death or imprisonment for life), and with no previous conviction, may be released on probation for good conduct instead of serving the sentence (in contrast, a man would have to be below 21 years of age to obtain this benefit; or, if over 21 years, to be convicted of an offence punishable with fine only or with imprisonment for seven years or less).

6. Section 416 enacts that if a woman sentenced to death is found to be pregnant, the High Court shall order the execution of the sentence to be postponed and may, if it thinks fit, commute the sentence to imprisonment for life.

Maharashtra Prison Manual, 1979

This has a separate chapter dealing with women prisoners. References to women are also found in other chapters. While it is not feasible to transcribe all these provisions here, the subjects covered are as follows: search, segregation, clothing, ornaments, facilities in barracks, pregnancy, childbirth, care of children of women prisoners, medical aid, interviews, limits of cellular confinement for women, educational and vocational training, release, women staff and their duties.

These provisions refer, on the whole, to convicted female prisoners, but would be applicable to undertrials confined in the women's section. Where undertrials are specifically mentioned, the regulations are generally inclusive of both men and women – contrasting the treatment of undertrials with that of convicts.

The term 'undertrial' is being used in this paper to refer to unconvicted persons in prison custody. "Undertrials are persons who are alleged to have committed offences under IPC and detained in prisons, facing a trial in a court of law."

The Model Prison Manual, 1976 defines undertrial as "a person who has been committed to pending trial or investigation by competent authority".[2]

The Bombay Jail Manual, 1935 describes that 'undertrial' and 'awaiting trial' are synonymous terms and refer to persons committed to prison whilst the charges against them are under judicial investigation.[3]

The long detainment of undertrials in the prisons is due to the slack procedures of the police in investigation of the cases and filing the chargesheets, and later of the courts in delaying the trials of the undertrial prisoners.

The problem of undertrials has posed a great challenge to the prison administration. Due to the increasing number of undertrial prisoners, the problem of overcrowding in prisons has reached unmanageable proportions. The large number of undertrials contribute of serious problems of congestion in prisons due to insufficient space and produces sub-human conditions of living.

Right from the introduction of modern prison system, undertrials are detained in the prison and are subjected to general prison discipline. Undertrial prisoners are generally confined in separate wards in district/central prisons. They are given more concessions than convicted criminal prisoners. The rules in the Maharashtra Prison Manual, 1979[4] make generous provisions to ensure that detention does not hamper the undertrial prisoner in preparing his/her defence. Specific legal and administrative provisions also exist with respect to women suspects and prisoners, which are intended to provide directions to the police, courts and prison authorities in the handling of the women prisoners.

Facilities Available for the Undertrial Women Prisoners

In general, the accused should be produced before a magistrate by the police within 24 hours from the time of her arrest, excluding the traveling time. At this time, the accused is said to be in/under police custody. If the police require the accused for further investigation, the magistrate can pass orders accordingly. If the police have completed their investigation, then, the magistrate can remand the accused to judicial or prison custody and is given a court date. If the accused is able to get out on bail, then, she must appear in court for her trial on the given date. But, if the accused is not able to get out on bail, she is detained in prison.

As an undertrial there are certain facilities available to a woman in prison. In Maharashtra, the following facilities are provided to women undertrial prisoners:

- In every prison, in which women are confined, there shall be one or more women jailors and/or matrons, who shall maintain discipline in the women's section of the prison. No woman undertrial shall be removed from the women's section except with the special permission of the superintendent and for the purpose of being taken to court, interviews, release or transfer.

- No male officers, including Superintendent and Deputy Superintendent, shall on any pretext enter the women's section without the women jailor or matron, and the two shall not separate while in the section.
- A register shall be maintained at the gate of the women's prison or women's section of a prison. Whenever any woman undertrial is taken out, an entry shall be made in the register. Whenever any visitor enters the section, an entry indicating name of the visitor, day and time of such visit, shall also be made in the register.
- Undertrial prisoners should be admitted during usual working hours of the prison. On admission they shall be examined by the medical officer for marks of violence, birth-marks, etc. And, a printed card should be sent to the undertrial's family giving information about the inmate's institutional number and address, brief summary of rules regarding interviews, letters, etc.
- It is the duty of every prison officer to find out whether an undertrial prisoner has been previously convicted and such information should be immediately forwarded to the concerned Superintendent of Police for necessary action.
- When an undertrial prisoner has been notified by the trying magistrate or the police as an approver or a confessing accused, she should be kept separate from others concerned in the same case.
- Children of women undertrials may be admitted if suitable arrangements for their care cannot be easily made outside.
- Private clothing to meet reasonable requirements should be allowed to undertrial prisoners. An undertrial prisoner, who has no sufficient clothing of her own, may be provided with the same at government cost.
- Food from outside may be allowed. Such prisoners shall not be served prison food. Undertrials should not be allowed to cook their food separately in the prison.

- Four letters per calendar month, two at the prisoner's cost, and two at the government cost, shall be allowed to be written by an undertrial. There shall be no limit on the number of incoming letters to prisoners.
- One interaction per calendar week with family members or relatives or close friends or lawyers may be allowed.
- No newspapers shall be supplied to undertrials at government cost.
- Unless so desires, no undertrial prisoner shall be allotted any work except that it shall be her duty to keep her bedding, clothing and yard clean.
- An undertrial prisoner may make purchases from the canteen as per canteen rules.
- Women undertrial prisoners should normally be escorted by women police. Separate conveyance also be provided for the transport of such prisoners.
- Every Prison Superintendent shall, on the first day of each month, submit to the Sessions Judge or the Chief Presidency Magistrate a statement of cases of all undertrial prisoners pending for more than three months in the court of the Judicial Magistrate.
- When an undertrial woman prisoner, accused of the offence of travelling ticketless, released on bail, she may be paid travelling allowance if the Superintendent considers it necessary her interest.
- As far as possible, women undertrial prisoners should be handed over to their relatives after release. If this is not possible, a police or prison guard should escort them to the nearest railway station or bus stand.

Children of the Women Undertrials

Women undertrials having children below four years of the age can keep them in the prison, while children above four years of age for whom no arrangements can be made outside, are placed in Children's Homes.

For the children, milk, banana and rice are provided. Medical facilities are also extended to them. But, there are no educational or recreational facilities available for these children.

To reduce the number of women undertrials, the Mulla Committee (also known as All India Committee on Jail Reforms, 1980–83) recommended that bail should be liberally granted to undertrials and those not able to furnish sureties should be released on personal recognition. The Probation of Offenders' Act should be extensively used for the benefit of women offenders in order to keep them away from prisons as far as possible.

Lacuna between the Declared Laws and Everyday Reality

The arrested person must be informed of the ground of his/her arrest, his/her right to bail and to engage a lawyer. But some officers are not conscious of their duty and they do not inform the accused of the grounds of his/her arrest.

When the police no longer require the individual for the purposes of investigation and if a prisoner is not released on bail, he/she is transferred to prison custody. In prison, the undertrial continues to be remanded and produced in court on the next date given. This process of giving remands may go on for weeks or months before the hearing actually starts.

As stated earlier, legal aid is the constitutional right of every suspect and free legal services can be provided to every accused person, who is unable to engage a lawyer and secure legal services on account of poverty or some other reason. State has to provide a lawyer to an accused person if the circumstances of the case and the needs of justice so require. But, it is totally at the mercy of the jail officers.

Right to speedy trial is recognized in Article 3 (i) of the Universal Declaration of Human Rights. It says that arrest and detention constitute restrictions on the right of personal freedom. Speedy trial is the essence of the criminal justice system. However, there is no specific criterion of promptness.

Liberty is a most valuable right and when the accused applies for bail, he/she seeks this right from the court. In offences which are specified in the code as bailable, bail is a matter of right. But most of the women undertrials are unaware of their legal rights.

The Indian Jail Committee (1919–20) stressed the need for proper classification of prisoners. Unfortunately, the arrested person has a right to be treated with human dignity and it is an offence for the police to inflict bodily pain on the individual. Custodial violence is a matter of concern. It is aggravated by the fact that it is committed by persons who are supposed to be the protectors of the citizens. Over the years, Police Commissions at national and state levels have been emphasizing the need to reform and humanize the police force. But, no concrete efforts have been made to implement them. Our jail manuals are outdated, our policemen are not trained in methods of interrogation, and have no access to scientific methods, which could automatically curtail the use of force. Suspects are picked up and detained for days and weeks, where the use of third degree methods is a common practice.

Conditions of Prisoners: Violation of Human Rights*

- Overcrowding is the most acute problem encountered by the inmates, and it goes usually to such an extent that the total number of inmates is almost four to five times the total capacity of the prison. The Jail Code allocates a space of 36 square feet to every prisoner, but prisoners hardly get it.
- The overall condition has adverse effect on the health and hygiene of the prisoners. Prison authorities failed to fulfil minimum standards set by UN. They also failed to ensure minimum floor space and lighting inside the prison.
- Proper meal is not provided to prisoners. The quality of food given to undertrials is not good. There is also discrimination in the food given to Indian women undertrials and the foreign women undertrials. The latter are provided with bread, eggs, more milk and other essentials. On the other

---

*Findings are based on the study of undertrial women prisoners of Arthur Road Central Prison, Mumbai conducted by the author.

hand, the locals have no such privilege because rules regarding food provisions prior to the pre-independence era are still in vogue. Food and meal timings are also not proper. (e.g., dinner would be given at 4.00 p.m.).

- An undertrial prisoner may make purchases from the jail canteen as per rules. But canteen coupons are sold only on the 1st and 15th of each month.
- The undertrials are not satisfied with the poor medical facilities. Even medicines provided are not effective.
- Women are also deprived of their basic needs, especially clothing and medical treatment.
- All undertrials are huddled together in the same barrack. Those suffering from contagious diseases have no separate arrangements. There is also no segregation of habitual from first offenders.
- Children below four years of the age can live with their undertrial mothers in the prison. But, in absence of proper and separate arrangements for the children in jail, they live in inhumane conditions.
- A feeling of isolation, insecurity, emotional imbalance and forced separation from family are largely felt by prisoners.
- There is also absence of comfort and a total absence of privacy, because of so many prisoners confined in a limited space.
- Women prisoners are usually subjected to physical and mental torture during police investigation. Some undertrials have even admitted being beaten up during interrogation by the police.
- Most of the women undertrials are uneducated and unaware of their legal rights. They are unable to defend themselves and are totally ignorant about the ways and means of securing legal help. They are unaware of the rules of remission or premature release and are at mercy of the officials.
- Lack of vocational training and leisure time leads to indiscipline. Lack of work for the inmates causes quarrels and fights among themselves. Even within an offender group, hierarchies exist. Prisoners presume themselves as superior

or inferior to others. Quarrelling and fighting among inmates and use of abusive language are a common feature in prison life.

- Undertrial prisoners are continuously anxious till someone comes to visit them or release them on bail. But, there are constraints and restrictions on the persons visiting the inmates. The relatives are permitted to visit only in the presence of an official so that close contact and free conversation is not possible. The visitors have to wait for hours outside before they are allowed to meet the prisoners for just five minutes.

Drawbacks of Existing Judicial Process

The criminal process beginning with arrests and ending in release and readjustment with society involves a lot of deprivation, including the deprivation of contacts with family members and the inevitable disruption of management and care of children. On the other hand, it is also true that the imprisonment of a woman is dysfunctional to her family and particularly to her children. So, they should be released on probation and allowed to live in their homes, because arrest and custody affects not only the undertrial prisoner in an advise manner, but also their family and children, in particular. The probation can prevent the both, viz., undertrial prisoner and her family, to suffer from social and psychological deprivation and also from the social stigma attached to imprisonment.

Imprisonment cannot be pleasing to anyone. There is no doubt that the removal of the offender from the family has a very serious and disabling impact on her family. One of the prison system's greatest failings is treating all insiders equally, because not every one in prison is a criminal. A major problem, which undertrial female prisoners, face is delayed trial period. It is not only criminal justice system, which is partial and silent about women but even outside its circle, society, family, religion are equally responsible for the present miserable conditions of women prisoners. For example, if family members are arrested for the same offence, the family spends more money and provide legal support to defend male relatives rather than female. In that case, female members stay in prison for long periods.

The National Expert Committee on Women Prisoners (1986–87), headed by Justice Krishna Iyer, was constituted in order to identify the gaps in or drawbacks of existing facilities and services and to evolve a more humane policy towards women offenders. The committee noted that existing malpractices in the various terms of custody affect women more adversely than men. Specific and specialized interventions are necessary to dispense custodial justice to woman and to protect her dignity and her person in custody. The committee has also proposed some interventions addressed to policy making, and reviewing enforcement of law.

Suggestions/Necessary Steps for Ensuring Human Dignity

To ensure human rights of the prisoners, there is a need of providing minimum conditions for ensuring human dignity. The right to live with human dignity is the fundamental right of every citizen. Following steps are necessary at different levels to improve the conditions and also to ensure human rights of the undertrial women prisoners:

Improvement in Criminal Justice Procedure

- Overcrowding of prisoners is due mostly to the large number of prisoners awaiting trial. Undertrial prisoners are retained in the prison for many months or years. So, alongside the expansion and modernization of prison facilities, there is also a crucial need for legal and judicial reforms. The government took up a programme in 1999 to reduce overcrowding in prisons, which is yet to come in force. With enhancing the capacity of prisons, as early as possible, undertrials should be brought into the judicial procedure and cases should be settled.
- Imprisonment stigmatizes persons. Most female criminals can easily be released on probation. This will also reduce overcrowding in prisons.

- More family courts should be established for the smooth and flexible administration of justice and for speedy disposal of the cases.
- During the training period police should be properly sensitized over issues related to women. The judges, magistrates and advocates require a thorough sensitization and orientation for more sensitive handling of judicial and legal procedures affecting women.

Improvement in Prison Facilities

- Prison must have congenial atmosphere. Prison authorities should behave properly and humanely.
- Improvement in daily facilities, cleanliness and hygiene education should be introduced and carried out with seriousness.
- The quality of food should be improved and the meal timings be made more suitable.
- Proper clothing should be provided for needy undertrial women prisoners.
- Proper medical facilities and medical examinations of women inmates should be ensured in prisons. Lady doctor should behave humanely and sympathetically.
- Prisoners shall be provided with water and such toilet articles as are necessary for health and cleanliness. The sanitary installation shall be adequate.
- Due regard should be paid to climatic conditions and particularly to cubic content of air, minimum floor space, lighting and ventilation.

Legal Aid

All women in custody must be informed of their rights in custody, including right to demand legal aid, if needed. Efforts should also be made to provide them legal aid. If the family of the prisoner has financial problems and is not able to arrange legal assistance, then, it may be made available either by prison authorities or NGOs. Legal counselling cells should be set up in every prison for women inmates.

Other Facilities

- A number of women prisoners suffer from mental depression and other forms of psychosomatic illness. There is hardly any arrangement for psychiatric treatment and counselling. For this, prison must appoint counsellors, social workers and also a qualified person with some knowledge of psychiatry.
- Recreational activities should be generated for women undertrials to reduce monotony in prison's life. The prisoners should also be engaged in work suitable to them for which they should be paid substantial wages.
- Prisoners should be allowed to send complaints against prison officials directly to the Ministry of Home Affairs without censorship by jail authorities.

Concluding Remarks

The criminal justice system is based on the principle that a person is innocent until proved guilty. The question that arises is why should people who are not convicted of a crime be incarcerated in inhuman conditions? Why should they be kept in prison for no other reason other than that they are suspected of having committed a crime?

The presence of excessive number of undertrials in prisons has created the situation of non-observance of human rights in prison. There are several prisoners awaiting their trial for years. The offences with which some of them are charged are trivial, which even if proved, would not warrant punishment for more than a few months. It is really regretting for the judicial system which permits incarceration of persons long periods without trial. We talk passionately about the protection and enforcement of human rights. But, are we not denying human rights to these persons, who are languishing in prisons for years for offences which perhaps they might ultimately be found not to have committed? Are we not withholding basic freedom from these neglected and helpless human beings who have been condemned to a life of imprisonment and degradation for years? Are speedy trials and freedom from detention not part of human rights? The time has come when the legal and judicial system has to be restructured so that such injustice does not occur.

Thus, the minimum standard rules should be implemented and the civic amenities required to sustain a human being should be assured for every prisoner. When persons are put behind the bars, it does not mean that they have lost their identity. They have been deprived of their valuable right of freedom of movement. So long as they possess human identity they have the right to have all the basic necessities and civic amenities assured by the Constitution and also by the Standard Minimum Rules of UN. The undertrial prisoners in no way should be subjected to deprivation of basic citizen's rights. Imprisonment within the walls of the prison is a rigorous punishment for a person. If in addition to this ordeal, basic necessities are inadequate, then we cannot call ourselves a civilized society.

Notes

1. Menon, N.R.M., "Legal Aid in the Criminal Proceedings", *Social Defence,* Vol. XIII, No.50, p.16.
2. The Model Prison Manual, 1976.
3. The Bombay Jail Manual, 1935.
4. Maharashtra Prison Manual, 1979.

References

Bhosle, Smriti. 2003. 'Undertrial Female Criminals in Mumbai City: A Sociological Study', unpublished Ph.D thesis, Shivaji University, Kolhapur.

Extracts from the Maharashtra Prison Manual, published by Vidhayak Sansad, Maharashtra and Human Rights Law Network, Mumbai, 1996.

Report of National Expert Committee on Women Prisoners, Vol. I & II, 1986–87, Ministry of Human Resource Development, Department of Women and Child Development, New Delhi.

Report of National Workshop on Custodial Justice to Women, National Institute of Public Co-operation and Child Development (NIPCCD), New Delhi, 1989.

9

Domestic Violence

Analysis of the Strategies

PRIYADERSHINI PAWAR

In almost all parts of the modern world, discrimination based on class, caste, race, nationality, colour, religion and the social and economic status is still predominant. Every minute there is a violation of human rights happening in India in various forms. In the Constitution of India, though men and women are endowed with equal rights, opportunities and justice, women are the 'weaker' section. Women have to still emerge in a male-dominated society. The religious and caste barriers have further obstructed them to walk with men. Large number of women are exploited and maltreated sexually, physically and even economically.

It is important here to clarify the concept of 'violence against women'. The United Nations Commission on the Status of Women defines violence against women to include, "any act of gender-based violence that results in, or is likely to result in, physical, sexual or psychological harm or suffering to women". The definition is understood to encompass, but not be limited to, physical, sexual, and psychological violence occurring in the family and outside it. Gender-based violence, including wife beating, rape, sexual abuse, and dowry-related murder is widely prevalent in India (Jejeebhoy, 1998). The data presented in Table 1 would give a clear idea of prevalence of violence against women:

Table 1

Crimes Against Women in India

Crime	*1991*	*1992*	*1993*	*1994*	*1995*	*1996*	*1997*
Rape	9,793	11,112	11,242	12,351	13,754	14,846	15,330
Abduction	12,300	12,077	11,837	12,998	14,063	14,877	15,617
Dowry deaths	5,157	4,962	5,817	4,935	5,092	5,513	6,006
Torture	15,949	19,750	22,064	25,946	31,127	35,246	36,592
Molestation	20,611	20,385	20,985	24,117	28,475	28,939	30,764
Sexual harassment	10,283	10,783	12,009	10,496	4,756	5,671	5,796
Importation of Girls	—	—	—	167	191	182	78
Sati	—	—	—	2	27	0	1
Immoral traffic	—	—	—	7,547	8,447	7,706	8,323
Indecent representation of Women	—	—	—	389	539	96	73
Total	74,093	79,037	83,954	98,942	1,06,471	1,13,076	1,18,580

Source: Crime in India, Ministry of Home Affairs, Government of India.

Two heads, 'dowry deaths' and 'torture' refer to cruelty by husband or his relatives specifically indicate what we may understand as domestic violence. This data relates to only registered crimes. A higher incidence of crime is often not viewed favourable by the authorities. There is a natural tendency to underreport crime. It means that in reality the rate of violence against women is higher than this. The data presented here shows that domestic violence is most prevalent in all types of crimes against women.

A term 'domestic violence' in the context of women includes various forms of violence that women face both in their natal and marital homes, at the hands of their father, brothers, sons, uncles, husband, and in-laws. Domestic violence can be physical, sexual, economic, emotional, verbal and psychological abuse. There are no commonly accepted definitions and methods of measuring the extent and intensity of this crime (*Saheli,* 2002).

Domestic violence cuts across class, caste and religious boundaries. It is one of the most powerful means of patriarchy to maintain the subordinate position of women. It is the crude use of force to put women in to a subordinate position. Violence is also used to pressurize women and their maternal family to fulfil dowry-related demands. In this way, domestic violence continues to keep millions of women in their subordinate positions within the family and in the society. Women thus become the instruments through which the social order reproduces itself and through which inequality is maintained (*Saheli,* 2002).

The above picture depicts the serious nature of domestic violence. As stated earlier, violence against women speaks in volume violation of human rights. Looking to the gravity of the domestic violence, the state and voluntary organizations have introduced some strategies to deal with the problem. But, it is necessary to analyse these strategies because the faulty strategies or inadequate response may be harmful to the victims. Hence, the objective of this paper is to analyze Family Counselling Centre (FCC) as one of the strategies to deal with the issue of domestic violence. It is done through having an idea about various legislative, state, voluntary and NGO strategies to deal with the problem of domestic violence. Further detailed information about the FCC is given with presentation and analysis of data collected from the FCC in Satara district. This includes how FCC functions, its work procedure, settings, staff pattern, factors that affect effective service system, etc. Finally, some suggestions are also given to improve the service delivery system of the FCC.

Strategies by State and NGOs

Actually, the state response to the problem of domestic violence came in around mid-eighties, after a sustained campaign on the issue of dowry-related violence. Since the police refused to register cases in the then existing provisions of the IPC, the demand was raised for a special enactment to deal with the issue. Two major changes that were brought out in 1983–84 were with regard to addition of Section 498 (A) and Section 304 (B) to the IPC (*Saheli,* 2002).

Besides legislative measures, the state and voluntary sector's response to deal with the problem of domestic violence came in the form of establishment of agencies such as Women's Police Stations, Police Counselling Cell, Special Cell for Women and Children, Family Court, Legal Aid Cells, Lok Adalats, Family Counselling Centres (FCCs), etc.

But, unfortunately, not a single person working in these agencies is well trained in counselling or helping women in crisis. They lack professionalism. The police personnel have their own style of dealing cases. Gender sensitivity is rarely found. Even legal agencies dealing with the issues related to domestic violence lack counselling skills. The FCC, which is obligatory for the training of its personnel, lacks necessary infrastructure and facilities too.

Despite talking loudly about equal rights, women are found everywhere as victims of violence. The beginning part of the paper gives some idea of this situation. The state and voluntary sectors are responding through several strategies as mentioned above. But, to really help victims of domestic violence, these strategies are inadequate and ineffective. Some of the strategies are made popular purposefully to show concern for women, but even they have not proved to be the real ones. However, the FCC has a lot of scope to provide good service to women in distress.

Following information about FCC would help us to understand present state, its potentialities and weaknesses. It would also help to take further measures to make this strategy fruitful to the sufferers of the domestic violence.

Family Counselling Centre

Family Counselling Centre (FCC) is the state response to domestic violence. It is a countrywide initiative taken jointly by the Central Social Welfare Board (CSWB) and the State Social Welfare Advisory Board (SSWAB) to counter family breakdowns.

The roots of this venture can be traced to the Voluntary Action Bureau (VAB) and various state boards established in 1982 by the CSWB at the national and state levels respectively. The idea was to help the government and voluntary organizations, through financial assistance, to specifically tackle crimes against women and children. Started as an experiment, the functioning of the VAB was extended for two years for the setting up of FCCs in the states. These initiatives were expected to provide preventive, referral and rehabilitative services to the victims of domestic violence and counselling in cases of 'marital maladjustment' (Poonacha and Pandey, 1999).

Some of FCCs are attached to the police stations. A few of them are even located within the premises of concerned police station and get then administrative support too. Police refer the cases related to domestic violence directly to FCC. The FCC funded by the CSWB is expected to be more professional compared to other agencies like Mahila Dakshta Samiti, Mahila Takrar Nivaran Kendra etc. As the CSWB has laid the condition to appoint trained and qualified counsellors (MSW, Psychologist, MA-Psychology etc.) only, the functioning of such FCCs is different and more systematic than other agencies.

FCC at Satara Police Station

The FCC named *Special Cell for Women and Children* was established in September 1998 at Satara Police Station in Maharashtra. An educational institute, a School of Social Work, runs this FCC having collaboration with the police department. The FCC has a regular staff of two counsellors (both female), a clerk and a peon. Both the counsellors are postgraduate in social work, age below 27 years and are unmarried, having one year experience before joining the FCC. They are all committed social workers. The FCC has separate advisory committee. The Superintendent of Police is the chairman of this committee. The members include District Government Pleader, Advocates, Psychiatrist, District Women and Children Officer, District Social Welfare Officer, District Publicity Officer, member of Alcoholic Anonymous, Principal and Lecturer of the Social Work College.

The Setting

The FCC operates from a separate room within the police station. The tables, chairs and cupboards are utilitarian, making the place look like a typical government office. There is no sufficient space for the clients to sit while waiting. They sit under the shade of a tree both in sunshine and rain. The staff however co-operates and shares the workload. Among the documents maintained by the FCC are (1) case files (with case history), (2) registers (comprising all the case registered at the FCC), (3) appointment diary, (4) half-yearly and annual reports (submitted to the CSWB, MSSWB) (5) correspondence registers, and (6) awareness programme reports etc.

Work Procedure

The FCC functions from Monday to Saturday from 10 a.m. to 5 p.m. Complaints from both the husband and wife are considered. The police refer the cases to FCC. In addition, sometimes, referrals are also made by advocates, mahila mandals, neighbours and old clients.

When a victim approaches the cell, his/her case typically goes through the following stages:

- Registration of complainant with case history
- Interview with complainant
- Calling the other party
- Interview with the other party
- Joint meetings with conflicting parties
- Home visits and investigation
- Arrival at compromise
- Follow-up and home visit

The first meeting is primarily intended to hear about the case and to assess the complexities involved in the client's expectations. Although in most cases the clients ask for mental and emotional support to women victims of physical violence, they are however unable to clearly articulate the means for fulfilling this need. The handling of the other party is also problematic . The counsellors follow the routine schedule of three notices to the other party to come and meet the counsellor. In most cases the parties do respond.

Effective counselling is conducted over a period of time and through many sessions: to begin with, the counsellor records the case history and makes a case file; subsequently, through various sessions, the counsellor enables the client to find solutions to her problems. It is aimed at providing the client with a supportive environment in which she could think of her options. Joint counselling sessions, with the spouse or in-laws (members involved in the problem) are also arranged.

In the case of default, the counsellor make home visits and involve the large kin network, neighbours of colleagues in persuading the concerned party to come to the counselling cell. A joint meeting is fixed on a mutually agreed time. Joint meeting may be a close door meeting between the counsellor and the couple only or may involve kin of the two sides. When a compromise is reached, the statements are recorded. The couples are advised to keep in touch and especially the victimized wife is assured that she can, in case the need arises in the future too, approach the cell any time for help. Even after compromise, counsellors wait for some months before closing a case. Personal home visits are also made from time to time.

Salary Pattern of the Staff

The staff is appointed on a purely temporary basis. They receive a consolidated monthly salary and do not enjoy any of the benefits of employment (such as gratuity, provident fund, increments or pension) available to the other government employees. Further, as shown in Table 2, their salaries are neither commensurate with their qualifications, nor the kind of services they provide in society. As the staff is unsure of their tenure and often think of moving out of their present jobs to other more remunerative ones, the only factor, which retains them in the FCC, is their commitment to their vocation.

Table 2

Salary Pattern of the Counsellors

Designation	*Consolidated Monthly Salary (Rs)*
Counsellor	2500
Clerk	1500
Attendant	500

Awareness Generation Programmes

The FCC arranges awareness generation camps for rural people, legal literacy camps, and youth's awareness programmes at the college level. The students from the schools of social work are also placed in the FCC for their fieldwork.

Supervision of the FCC

The Central Social Welfare Board (CSWB) and the Maharashtra State Social Welfare Advisory Board (MSSWAB) monitor functions of the FCC and also provide guidance from time to time. Annual and half-yearly reports are submitted to the CSWB and to the MSSWAB regularly. The advisory committee meeting is held with FCC staff once in every three months, wherein administrative matters and case details are discussed.

Trainings for Staff Development Programmes

The CSWB organizes training for FCC staff in counselling and other related areas such as women's issues, family, and law etc. They are also given guidance on the administration of their respective centres.

Nature of the Complaints

Majority of complaints registered in the FCC are made by female members. These are mainly about maladjustment with spouse, due to harassment, suspicious nature, addiction, extramarital relations, economic crises, sexual problems, interference of parents of spouse, etc. Some other cases are quarrel among brothers, sisters, siblings and parents, relatives, property matters, neighbours, etc.

The progress report of the FCC is about the outcome of these cases. Reconciliation and non-reconciliation of the cases is clearly shown. Other cases are referred to the various agencies like Free Legal Aid, Police, Short Stay Home, Alcoholic Anonymous, Psychiatrist, etc. Some of the cases are referred to more than one agency.

Table 3

Five Year's Progress Report of the FCC

Nature of Cases	*1998–1999*	*1999–2000*	*2000–2001*	*2001–2002*	*2002–2003*
Dowry demand	1	1(0.86%)	1	7(3%)	4
Marital maladjustment with					
spouse	26(20%)	9(8%)	22(18%)	22(10%)	16(12%)
in-laws	8(6%)	7(6%)	11(9%)	12(6%)	4(3%)
Maladjustment due to					
personality differences	12(9%)	5(4%)	6(5%)	5(2%)	7(5%)
interference of parents	3(2%)	1	2(2%)	4(2%)	3(2%)
interference of in-laws	8(6%)	28(25%)	25(20%)	22(10%)	2(1%)
Extramarital relations	14(11%)	5(4%0	3(2%)	20(9%)	5(4%)
Addiction	18(14%)	23(20%)	25(20%)	44(21%)	23(17%)
Economic crisis	6(5%)	3(3%)	3(2%)	2(0.8%)	5(4%)
Any other	34(26%)	31(27%)	24(20%)	37(18%)	65(%)
Total	130	113	122	210	134

Table 4

Outcomes of the Cases in Five Years

Nature of Cases	*1998–1999*	*1999–2000*	*2000–2001*	*2001–2002*	*2002–2003*
Reconciliation	82(63%)	65(56%)	73(60%)	180(77%)	114(82%)
Non-reconciliation	9(7%)	22(19%)	17(14%)	46(22%)	20(15%)
Legal aid	2(2%)	2(2%)	2(2%)	4(2%)	4(3%)
Police case	5(4%)	7(6%)	12(10%)	17(8%)	12(9%)
Short stay home	2(2%)	2(2%)	6(5%)	1(0.4%)	1(0.7%)
Alcoholic anonymous	13(10%)	14(12%)	15(12%)	18(9%)	13(10%)
Court cases	10(8%)	1(0.8%)	1(0.8%)	9(4%)	9(7%)
Psychiatrist	—	—	—	—	2

Note: Some cases are referred at multiple sources.

Analysis of Data

From 1998 to 2003, during the period of five years, some 709 cases have been registered. Considering the data, majority of cases are under the headings – *marital maladjustment with spouse, maladjustment due to interference of in-laws, addiction, and any other.*

The 'marital maladjustment with spouse' is due to harassment, cruelty, torture, etc. The addiction cases are mostly of alcoholic nature and under the title 'any other' various types of cases are registered, like one-sided love affair, quarrels between brothers, sisters, parents and siblings. Sometimes cases regarding quarrels between neighbours etc. are also registered. Extramarital relations of the husband, alcoholism and personality problems like suspicious nature are the chief reasons for violence. Dowry-related problems are relatively less significant in the cases that come to the counselling centre.

The most important and interesting component of this data is about the status of outcome after the FCC intervention. The reconciliation rate is quite high. The minimum and maximum rate of reconciliation is 56 per cent and 82 per cent respectively, whereas the total percentage of the reconciliation during five years is 70 per cent.

So far as the non-reconciliation rate is concerned, it is minimum of 7 per cent to maximum of 22 per cent. These cases are generally sent back to the police. The cases referred to the Free Legal Aid Centre are shown under title 'Legal Aid', the clients who approach to the court on their own are shown under the title, 'Court Cases'. Such cases are minimum 0.8 per cent to maximum 8 per cent during the period of five years. The alcoholic persons are referred to the Alcoholic Anonymous. Majority of the cases are from lower and lower-middle income groups, living in slums and the nearby villages.

Shortcomings of the FCC: Some Suggestions

Shelter Home

The FCC has no shelter home, short stay home or any alternative arrangement. It has no extra funds other than counsellors' salary and administrative expenses. Women in the crisis situations rush to the FCC and are generally not willing to go back. Not sure of the parental support these women do not even prefer to go there. At such times temporary shelter is required for them. As shelter arrangement is not available, the victimized woman is sent back to her in-laws house and has to stay in the same environment till the joint meeting is arranged. Only in accused members are called serious cases the immediately for discussion with the help of police. But, in these cases also, counsellors try for the reconciliation or it can be said that reconciliation is imposed upon them because of lack of shelter.

The victim of domestic violence is aware of the fact that in case she does not get support from her parents, no temporary shelter will be made available to her by the state or NGOs. In such situation, if she is economically not independent, then, she has to return back to the same environment hoping for the best.

The FCC refers some cases to the short stay home, which is some 100 km away from the town. Hence, all the time, it is not convenient to refer cases to the short stay home. Also, the environment of this short stay home is not congenial.

Currently, the SWB funds counselling cells and short stay homes under various schemes. There is also need for funding the emergency shelter needs of women approaching SWB counselling cells. Such centres may provide shelter for a night or two to the needy women who are presently turned away for lack of availability of such accommodation.

Vocational Training Centre

The high rate of reconciliation in the FCC is again a matter to be thought on. In many cases women do not want to continue their miserable married life but due to the economic dependence on husband, they have to do so and are compelled for reconciliation. Actually, the FCC should have a good vocational training centre of its own or be linked with such centres to arrange training and income generating programmer to make woman economically independent.

Travel and Food

When women visit the FCC and have no money to come back, FCCs have no funds to arrange for their travel and food. However, the FCC at Satara collects some donations to provide food and travelling expenses to women in distress/need.

Fixed Working Hours

The FCC has fixed office timings (10 a.m. to 5 p.m.). In reality, the FCC should be open for 24 hours in shifts, because women in crisis cannot wait till it opens. FCC needs more staff to pay full attention to the clients, make home visits, and keep follow up to give real service to women.

Sufficient Space and Childcare Facility

One more constraint in the adequate functioning of the FCC is lack of space. FCC has a single room only. No separate room is available for counselling sessions or for the clients to wait. When the family counselling sessions are conducted, it causes inconvenience.

Further, there are no childcare facilities. Women with children are compelled to leave them with some relative or friend when they come to the FCC. If they bring them, they have no option but to talk about their problems in their presence.

Salaries and Service Conditions of the FCC

As stated earlier, the FCC staff is recruited on purely temporary basis with very low salary. The staff is unsure of their tenure and often thinks of moving out of their present job to other more remunerative ones. SWB has made it mandatory for employing only qualified postgraduates (MSW, MA-Psychology) for the post of counsellors. This, along with a very low salary, has made it imperative for them to employ fresh postgraduates without any experience. The counsellors appointed in the FCC are unmarried and are less than 30 years of age. Most of the times the fresh social work students or with one to two years of experience join FCC as a counsellor. Experienced people either do not have a required degree or expect more salary. This term of recruitment of counsellor affects on the appointment of the experienced persons for good counselling practice. Inexperienced, not sufficiently trained young counsellors without much exposure to women's problems, are unable to respond to the victims of the domestic violence. Unmarried counsellors do feel embarrassment in dealing problems of sexual nature.

Training of FCC Counsellors

Presently, there is lack of comprehensive training programme for counsellors. The training courses available at present are of very short duration of just four to ten days. The current programmes are too theoretical and far from realities. The counsellors require more regular and thorough training. The training programme should have different modules on the counselling skills, psychological techniques, legal literacy and therapies to deal with domestic violence, gender sensitivity, changing laws and such current information.

Inadequate Staff

The FCC attached to the Satara police station gets a vast number of clients whereas the staff provided to deal with them is not adequate. Two counsellors remain busy in listening to the dealing complaints, maintaining records, home visits and dealing with correspondence. In this situation, it is also difficult to maintain one's mental and physical health. The clerk and attendant in many FCCs are busy with the organization's other work. Hence, counsellors perform all the duties, which is taxing on them. They feel exhausted and at a time find that they are not receptive to the clients. They need change in the routine work, especially from continuously listening complaints of harassment, torture, quarrels and violence.

Publicity

There is need to publicize the FCC programme through local newspapers, radio and television. The SWB should take initiative to do adequate publicity to reach the needy. At present, such efforts to inform the public about the institution have been ineffective. Handbills, pamphlets and awareness camps are the other means for exposure.

Conclusion

From state to NGO, from legislative to the FCC, different strategies are developed to deal with the issue of domestic violence. Preventive, supportive and rehabilitative strategies are also developed to deal with the issue to help women victims grappling with the problem. Strategies such as the FCC provide only supportive help and are therefore inadequate. Due to this, reconciliation is forced on women. The principal shortcoming has been the NGO sector's limited success in offering suitable alternatives to women other than resettling in a violent home. Victimized women are sent back to the same unsafe place. Hence, such faulty strategies again violate human rights. Therefore, it is necessary to look at this issue with this angle. Lots of further efforts are required to make these strategies complete, which would really give justice and human rights to women.

To achieve rehabilitation and prevention, some of the suggestions stated in the paper like short stay home, vocational training, etc., may be considered. For the prevention of the domestic violence, programmes like pre-marital sex education in schools and colleges, and workshops for parents should be organized by FCCs. The problems of delay in getting justice, follow ups of the legal cases, legal awareness etc. are also important.

References

Ahuja, Ram. 1997. *Social Problems in India.* Jaipur: Rawat Publications.

Bhattacharya, Sanjay. 2003. *Social Work: An Integrated Approach*. New Delhi: Deep and Deep.

Fifth Annual Report, Special Cell for Women and Children, Satara Police Station, Satara Looking at Domestic Violence: January-April 2002,' A Saheli Presentation', *Saheli* Newsletter.

Jejeebhoy, Shireen. 1998. 'Wife-Beating in Rural India: A Husband's Right? Evidence from Survey Data', *Economic and Political Weekly*, 855–862.

Mitra, Nishi. 2000. 'Domestic Violence as a Public Issue: A Review of Responses'. Mumbai: TISS.

Poonacha, Veena and Pandey, Divya. 1999. 'Responses to Domestic Violence in the State of Karnataka and Gujarat'. Mumbai: SNDT.

10

Women's Rights and the Question of Culture

The Ho Tribe of Jharkhand

RITAMBHARA HEBBAR

The paper addresses the issue of gender and human rights in a community known to have been a part of the tribal movement that had resisted the violation of its rights by the state. The Ho tribe, as one of the dominant tribes within Jharkhand, was in the forefront of the movement for a separate tribal state of Jharkhand.[1] The Ho are largely concentrated in the West Singhbhum district of Jharkhand.[2] Jharkhand, which was formed in November 2000, was carved out of Bihar after over fifty long years of struggle.[3] The movement had campaigned against the violation of their rights on land and forests, which the movement argued, had simultaneously led to the deterioration of the natural environment. In presenting a systematic critique of state institutions and practices around land and forests, it made a case of possessing ecologically viable and friendly knowledge systems and practices that could restore the ecology. Thus, it not only brought to light the importance of respecting the rights of the community vis-à-vis the state, but also presented an alternative to restoring the natural environment.

The claim of possessing a more humble and egalitarian alternative relationship with nature as against the one pursued by the modern state acquires authenticity from the lives and work of the forest dwellers in the area, prominently women. The description of everyday life and work of the Ho on land and forests as well as community life cannot proceed without an enunciation of women's contribution to the same (Hebbar, 2005). Women's work and their role as primary agents of socialization are fundamental in establishing and renewing this special relationship to land and forests, wherein it is difficult to separate economic labour from the symbolic capital that goes in to maintaining the home, the community, land and forests. Land and forests are the media through which the tribes relate to the phenomena of life and death and deliberate on who they are and what is to become of them. They are a part of their cosmology and therefore integral to a sense of self. Thus, the issue is not only about how much labour is put in, but also the kind of labour involved. And, it is this relationship that, the movement argues, sets apart tribal understanding of land and forests from the scientific, modern management of resources.

Women's contribution to the Jharkhand movement has also been tremendous, as evident in the number of grassroots women's organizations spread all over Jharkhand. The All India Conference of Women Organizations held in Ranchi in 1997 was fully represented by organizations from Jharkhand working in the grassroots such as Jharkhand Mahila Sangharsh Samiti based in Ranchi, Shramjivi Mahila Samiti (Jamshedpur). Mahila Samakhya (Ranchi), Badlav (Dumka), Visthapit Sanghatan Sangh (Ichagarh), Nari Mukti Vahini (Palamau), Aqua (Giridih), Sanyukt Mahila Samiti (West Singhbhum) and Koel-Karo Jan Sanghatan (West and East Singhbhum), Some of the major issues raised by these organizations were regarding their resentment over irrigation projects (such as Ichagarh Dam Project), field firing ranges (Netrahaat), bauxite mines and white stone factories (Palamau and West Singhbhum), abuse of women workers in brick kilns and coal mines spread all over Jharkhand and out-migration of women of the area and their initiation into the illicit profession of flesh trade. The large turnout of women in the conference and of organizations working on issues of displacement demonstrated the active engagement and prominent role of women in the movement.

As a community that has been a victim of human rights violation by the state as well as having had women as equal participants in the struggle, and as custodians of the ecologically viable forms of natural resource management that the movement so proudly proclaims as its own, it is ironical that it has been reticent in addressing the issue of gender rights within the community. The specific reference here is to the issue of granting land rights, or rights to inheritance, to Ho women. There has been, for almost a decade now, a debate over granting land rights to women among the Ho tribe of West Singhbhum, Jharkhand. The issue of women's rights on land amongst the Ho came up before the formation of Jharkhand, at a time when the movement was trying to strengthen its base by forging a collective identity within tribes and of all tribes in the area. A woman activist, who filed a case in the Supreme Court demanding inheritance rights on land for Ho women, brought it up for debate.[4] This sparked off tensions in the area and lent itself to a long-lasting debate over the intention behind it.

In the following section, I present some of the popular arguments raised within the Ho community against granting land rights to Ho women. Most of the arguments presented against granting inheritance rights to women deliberate on what would happen to the community once the right to inheritance were granted to women. The focus then is not so much on women in as much as it is a concern for the community, as to how it would make the community more vulnerable vis-à-vis the rest of society (the non-tribe) and the state. The question of import here however is whether the right to practise one's culture forecloses a possibility of dialogue on social justice within a community, which has clearly accepted the value of social justice in relation to its right against the state. What suddenly makes the community sacrosanct when the issue is of pursuing social justice within its confines? Is the issue of rights distinct from the issue of responsibilities and justice? How are we to then address the issue of gender justice within the human rights framework? The paper does not attempt to provide answers to the questions posed, which are highly complex and delicate in nature, but rather seeks to break ground by addressing issues of social justice in marginalized communities without seeming to alienate their struggle for self-rule.

The Debate on Land Rights

The popular opinion has been against granting inheritance rights on land to women.[5] The general perception is that the hullabaloo over the same is a ploy of the *dikus* (outsiders or non-tribes; the class of industrialists, merchants and traders) to weaken the community from within by creating tensions between the men and women of the community.[6] Another major reservation with granting inheritance rights to women has been that it would lead to the disintegration of the community. Since the Ho are patrilineal and virilocal and women are constantly on the move through marriage, the argument is that land rights to women would be meaningless as they would not stay at a place in order to cultivate the land they claim. And, on the other hand, if women do decide to exercise this right, it would lead to confusion in the existing system of marriage and descent and lead to the break up of the patrilineage, on the basis of which all Ho villages have been settled.

The Ho land system is founded on the *khuntkatti* system. The word *khunt*, which stands for the patrilineal descent group, is originally Munda, adopted by the British for administrative purposes.[7] The word for the patrilineal descent group in Ho is *killi*. The term *khuntkatti* is a conjunction of two words, *khunt* and *kati*, which translates in English as the 'the patrilineal descent group' and 'to clear land' respectively. Amongst the Ho, prominence is given to the patrilineage whose ancestor was the first clearer of land and was responsible for establishing the village. In 1920, with the Tuckey settlement, the British extended the Chotanagpur Tenancy Act, 1908 amongst the Ho. They converted this privileged social status of the Khuntkattidars (the descendants of the first clearer of land) into a legal one. Thus patriliny was consolidated with the extension of the Chotanagpur Tenancy Act of 1908 to Singhbhum in 1920. It thereby also introduced a legal distinction between the descendants of the Khuntkattidar and the descendants of the later settlers known in British records as the *parja* (also translates as subjects or ordinary people).

Although this distinction was made for determining land rights, the term *'Khuntkattidar'* gradually came to be associated with persons of superior derivation and descent. It is worth noting here that it is the Khuntkattidars that primarily hold large plots of land and the legislation will directly affect their interests than the others, who are not privileged either in terms of the acres of land they hold or in terms of being granted any protection by law. This observation is pertinent in the context that if the bill were passed, it would also benefit Khuntkattidar women married to Ho men belonging to the *parja* category. The law thereby can well become a channel for social and economic mobility among the Ho and in the process upset the existing social and economic hierarchies within the community.

The existing pattern of landholding, it is argued, encourages social ties of the patrilineage (*killi*) whereas the women's rights to inheritance would undermine it. The latter would lead to fragmentation of land and the disintegration of the family as a unit. Besides of course presuming the functional utility of the patrilineage in maintaining unity among the Ho, this belief excludes or underplays the role of women in the maintenance of the social order. Although a patrilineal system vests authority and property in the hands of men, the system is not synonymous with men alone. The contest for control, as it is played out among the Ho, seems to be between men and women. However, this is not the case. Different women may have different stakes in patriarchy. Gender dynamics are most often than not played out in conjunction with other factors of class, status and power. Therefore, to associate giving inheritance rights to women, as an attack on the patrilineage and concurrently on the community (of men), is indeed dramatic.

Also, this leads us to another issue of theoretical and methodological significance in connection with women land rights. The terms 'family' and 'household' have been regularly examined as units of sociological analyses, especially in the context of devaluation of women's work as well as the non-recognition of women's labour in the household (Shah, 1973, 1998; Saradamoni, ed., 1992). On the one hand, the term 'family' has been dissociated from the term 'household' in that the household is the residential unit or the living arrangement of the family (Shah, 1973). On the other hand, the census operations have not paid much attention to the two terms and have restricted its utility to data collection for population surveys (Rao in Saradamoni, ed., 1992). The two terms have been used interchangeably. Either way, the conceptual differences have not contributed favourably towards recognition of women and women's work as integral to its definition. The separation of the terms 'household' and 'family' might have helped in recognizing and documenting the various changes in the constitution of a household in or over a region, caste and community, but has retained the patriarchal definition of a family thereby reducing the former as a deviation vis-à-vis the latter. The household, as a practical variant of the category 'family', poses no threat to the structural definition of the family, as a patrilineal, patrilocal unit, under a patriarchal head with all ritual, social and economic rights vested in the male members. "The law is concerned primarily with the constitution of the property holding group and with the persons having rights of maintenance from the property-holding group, and not with the constitution of the household group" (ibid: 55). In the process, the divide between family and household undermines the role and contribution of women in community life and perpetuates the myth of women as appendages.

The fear that the patrilineage would break down affecting village and family life if women do decide to claim rights on land and stay back in their natal homes to cultivate it. This does not hold ground in the light of some of the changes that have been observed among the Ho and other communities in the organization of agriculture. A study on a Rajasthan village revealed that with the growing demand for labour due to the out-migration of men, there has been a demographic shift in the village and changes in kinship practices. More and more married women return to their natal homes to assist during the agricultural season and that there has been a reduction of the distance between women's natal and conjugal residence over the years (Palriwala in Sangari and Chakravarti, eds., 1999). This seriously questions the assumption that once married, women are permanent residents of their conjugal homes and thereby also the fear that property rights to women and their consequent mobility for managing agricultural work on land will lead to the disintegration of the family as a unit. The experience of villages in West Singhbhum is similar in that many Khunkattidar men have taken up jobs in the railways and the numerous mines that have mushroomed all over West Singhbhum. Many of them prefer to stay at their place of work than commute great distances for work every day. The responsibility of agricultural work then falls primarily on women. In such a scenario, women's regular presence is what sustains work on land and the domestic unit within the village. It is men's mobility in fact that threatens the survival of the domestic unit and agricultural work. In many households, young unmarried daughters as well as married daughters supervise agricultural work and contribute their labour towards their natal home. The mobility or permanency of women are contingent factors and cannot be the standard criterion for conferring or denying land rights to women.

Also, high incidences of land transfers from tribes to non-tribes, despite regulations that restrict such transfers, have been another cause for concern (Xaxa, 2004: 362). According to some scholars, non-tribal men accomplish these transfers by marrying tribal women, in a rather surreptitious manner, to avoid legal implications (Singh, 1988). Granting of land rights to women, it is argued, would only make matters worse, as then the transfers would be legal and direct. It is worth noting here that these land transfers occurred not *because* of women's rights on land, so to argue that the latter will be the *cause* for further transfers is hypothetical. Moreover, the objection to granting land rights to women was also passed off as a concern for their safety; non-tribal men may marry them to only abandon them later. They may even exploit them and harass them for more money. The central concern in this entire deliberation is land; the right of women is not the subject of deliberation. At the most, the concern for women is paternalistic. Rights of women are not only secondary to the community, but are set against it; as what is seen as getting violated here is the rights of the community vis-à-vis the *dikus*, with tribal women almost supplementing their intentions. The debate then has become another instance of the community's experience with persecution and discrimination. The key concern is yet again the right to one's culture and way of life.

Which Culture Are We Talking About?

The human rights discourse has been shaky on the issue of the rights of a community over its culture, as it often comes in direct conflict with the human rights of an individual. The rights of a community to practise its culture relativizes the inalienable and indivisible character of human rights guaranteed to every individual. The issue of women rights has further complicated matters. Feminists do not view the issue of women's rights within the purview of individual rights, that is, individual women clamouring for greater autonomy within the community or against the state. Women's rights are rights of a community of women, universally oppressed and marginalized. Thereby, there has been an attempt to essentialize the experiences of women across the categories of caste, class, region and race. This perspective has faced criticism on the grounds that the experience of gender is mediated by other forms of discrimination and therefore cannot be presented as an exclusively women's issue. Feminist scholars have been uneasy over what they call the 'hierarchization of oppression', wherein the contest is over determining as to which oppression is greater (that of race, caste, class or gender) and therefore acquires precedence in redress (Parashar in Kapur, ed., 1996). This singular dissection of women's experience with 'other things being equal' is as unrealistic as the position that homogenizes women's experiences across cultures. Clearly, just as there is plurality in women's experience of oppression and subjugation, there are plural experiences of culture and community across class, caste, colour and gender that needs to be understood and highlighted to make a case for various women's voices.

This debate is of interest to us here, especially in the light of the fact that the issue of women's land rights among the Ho did not elicit strong support from ordinary Ho women, except for a handful of these women who have been actively campaigning for women's rights in the area. The question often asked in various public discussions was as to what right do non-Ho women have to interfere in a community matter. The question was brought up by a number of erudite Ho women, who felt that they had relatively greater freedom and were better off in their community in comparison to the neighbouring caste Hindu women. The answer to this question is tricky and unwieldy, and may well lead one to ask whether one can then ever represent the 'other'. Rather than going in circles over the issue of rights, the possible route to disentangling the issue of women's rights versus community rights could be of seeking out the terms of the debate that reveal the indeterminate nature of the interests so vehemently defended within the community.

There is a repeated reference to 'culture' or a 'way of life', which is sought to be protected and sheltered from 'outsiders' and outside influences. Interestingly, the reference to 'culture' and 'way of life' in the debate on land rights to women is qualitatively different in form and content from what was presented as a part of the claim to self-rule. While the initial reference to culture was inclusive of women and derived its legitimacy as much from women's work and life, the latter is estranged from women's lives and role in the maintenance of the community. This calls into question the very definition of culture and its importance in the assertion of self-rule and autonomy. All these terms, 'culture', 'way of life' and 'outsiders' are essentialized and fixed in the vocabulary of resistance, which translates these terms into a divide between us versus them, that is, tribe versus diku, self versus other, and community versus state. The legislation is seen as attacking not only the existing pattern of land inheritance, but also devaluing the authority of the community over its members to convene on, redefine and fix matters of culture and tradition. Thus, what the community really seeks to challenge is the state's authority as the 'sole giver of values' and in the process seeks to *organize* and *fix* culture so as to provide an alternative set of values (Das, 1996). In fixing culture through a set of values, norms and practices, the community replicates the ways of the state by restricting dialogue within its confines. Here, the term 'culture' performs a political function of seeking immunity from outside interference and of the state. Tribe, self and the community are then sought to be homogenized into an integrated whole, and the class and gender differences and hierarchies are disregarded to present a univocal voice of the community.

The Ho Samaj Mahasabha, a social organization comprising of influential members (mostly Khuntkattidars) of the Ho community, has been active in the area in redefining and fixing customs among the Ho. The Mahasabha has come out with a calendar in its attempt to fix the date of festivals, and holidays, which as of now is not decided uniformly across the community and differs from village to village. Likewise, it has fixed the amount of brideprice payable to the bride's family, which till now was left to the discretion of the latter. The Mahasabha, however, has been silent on the issue of gifts given by the bride's side to the bridegroom's family. In its justification of polygamy as a practice to fulfil a desire for a male heir (which is not always the case), it reinstates the importance of a son over a daughter among the Ho.[8] The Mahasabha also encourages arranged marriage or 'social' marriages as they are called among the Ho marriages by choice, which is common in the villages, especially among the *parjas* or the lower classes among the Ho, as they can ill-afford the expenses and fanfare that accompany 'social' marriages.

Clearly, at the receiving end of this tussle for control then is the lingering organic and unprompted form of culture, and which formed the reason for the struggle for self-rule in the first place and, that has, till now, outlived the various attempts to contain it. Thus, instead of locating the debate on women's right within the discourse of community versus the state, wherein the community is seen as 'preserving' its culture, it would be fruitful to relocate it within the larger contested domain of redefining and fixing culture of the community. Ho Samaj Mahasabha is only one of the contenders of culture, in its attempt to redefine and fix cultural practices and traditions. Then again, if the rights of women have to be addressed within the community, it has to be placed within this space of 'recall', wherein tradition and culture are being redefined as well as contested in the context of their contemporary struggle for self-rule.

Conclusion

The debate on women's land rights among the Ho brings to the fore the general problems faced by the women's movement in addressing women's issues in marginalized communities, religious and ethnic minorities. The debate focuses on women rather than the issue of rights; on whether women deserve the rights they demand. This not only goes against the fundamentals of human rights, but also reveals how the issue of rights without a commitment to social justice can be unequal and abusive. The challenge then, in the context of gender and human rights, is as to how to weave social justice within the framework of rights, and make communities responsible for the rights they seek in their quest for self-rule.

Notes

1. The movement demanded a state comprising the tribal districts within the state of West Bengal, Madhya Pradesh, Orissa and Bihar, which corresponds to the geographical division of the Chotanagpur plateau. The Chotanagpur plateau is known for its ecological and cultural diversity; both for its forest and mineral resources, and for the different tribes that inhabit the area. The 1961 census lists 29 tribes within Chotanagpur, which are Asur, Baiga, Banjara, Bathudi, Binjhia, Birhor, Birjia, Chero, Chik-Baraik, Gond, Gorait, Ho, Karmali, Kharia, Kharwar, Khond, Kisan, Kora, Korwa, Lohra, Mahli, Mal-Paharia, Munda, Oraon, Parhaiya, Santhal, Sauria Paharia and Savar.
2. The Ho are a part of the Austro-Asiatic group and belong to the larger Munda-speaking family, which also includes the Santhal, Munda and the Kharia.
3. Jharkhand, as we know it today, is a truncated form of the originally proposed state by the members of the movement and includes only the eighteen tribal districts within Bihar. These 18 districts are Godda, Sahebganj, Pakaur, Dumka, Deoghar, Dhanbad, Bokaro, Giridih, Hazaribagh, Kodarm, Chatra, Palamau, Garhwa, Lohardaga, Gumla, Ranchi, East Singhbhum and West Singhbhum. The tribal districts of West Bengal (Purulia, Bankura and Birbhum), Orissa (Sambhalpur and Sundergarh) and Madhya Pradesh (Raigarh and Surguja) have been left out of the State. Instead, four new districts have also been created in Jharkhand. They are Latehar (out of Palamau), Simdega (out of Gumla), Saraikela (out of West Singhbhum), and Jamtara (out of Dumka).
4. See Ahuja (1997: 211–14) for details of the Public Interest Litigation filed by Madhu Kishwar against the State of Bihar challenging sections, 7,8 and 76 of the CNT Act of 1908, which determines land holding pattern in the area.

5. The arguments against the bill were gathered in the course of my research among the Ho, between 1996–8, which came up in various fora such as conferences, informal discussions, and public debates.
6. Although the term 'diku' in its simplest meaning refers to 'outsiders' or to the non-tribal population, it was initially inducted into official vocabulary by the British wherein they kept a record (known as the Diku Reports), during each settlement, of the number of outsiders who migrated into Singhbhum. The diku were looked upon with suspicion and were associated with fraud and deception. In as much as the diku were responsible for a number of illegal activities in the area, the construction of the diku as the 'conniving' outsider served the British well, as it helped them to project themselves as the benefactors of the Ho. The term however gained greatest significance in the Jharkhand movement. It not only identified the 'outsider' in the merchant, industrialist and the bureaucrat, but also encapsulated the experiences and processes of exploitation of tribes in the region.
7. *Kati* has two meanings in Ho: a sharp blade, usually attached to the natural spurs of a cock for fighting, and to put something horizontal.
8. "When a boy is born, it is said that *jang* or *bone* is born, that is, a person who is strong and the backbone of the society whereas the birth of a girl is termed as *udal-padal* or other." A common example cited by Jharkhandi women activists in the All India Conference of Women's Organizations working in the grassroots held in Ranchi in 1997 to illustrate the position of the girl child among them.

References

Ahuja, Sangeeta. 1997. *People, Law and Justice: Casebook on Public Interest Litigation*. Vol. I. Delhi: Orient Longman Ltd.

Das, Veena. 1996. 'Cultural Rights and the Definition of Community', in Upendra Baxi and Oliver Mendelsohn (eds.). *The Rights of Subordinated Peoples*. pp. 117–158. New Delhi: OUP.

Deeney, J., S.J. 1978. *Ho Grammar and Vocabulary*. Chaibasa: Xavier Ho Publications, St. Xavier's High School.

Hebbar, Ritambhara. 2005. 'Homecoming: Ho Women, Work and Land Rights in Jharkhand'. *Sociological Bulletin*, Vol. 54, No. 1, January–April, pp. 18–39.

Kelkar, G. and D. Nathan. 1991. *Gender and Tribe: Women, Land and Forests in Jharkhand*. Delhi: Kali for Women.

Kishwar, Madhu. 1987. 'Toiling Without Rights: Ho Women of Singhbhum', *Economic and Political Weekly*. Vol. 22, No. 3, 4 and 5, pp. 95–101, 149–55 and 194–200.

Lorduswamy, Stan. 1997. *Jharkhandi's Claim for Self-Rule*. Delhi: Indian Social Institute and BIRSA.

Palriwala, Rajni. 1996. 'Negotiating Patriliny: Intra-Household Consumption and Authority in Northwest India'. *In* Rajni Palriwala and Carla Risseeuw (eds.) *Shifting Circles of Support: Contextualizing Gender and Kinship in South Asia and Sub-Saharan Africa*. New Delhi: Sage Publications. pp. 190–218.

—. 1999. 'Transitory Residents, Invisible Workers: Rethinking Locality and Incorporation in a Rajasthan Village'. *In* Kumkum Sangari and Uma Chakravarti (eds.) *From Myths to Markets: Essays on Gender*. Delhi and Shimla: IIAS and Manohar Publications. pp. 237–73.

Parashar, Archana. 1996. 'Essentialism or Pluralism: The Future of Legal Feminism'. *In* Ratna Kapur (ed.) *Feminist Terrains in Legal Domains: Interdisciplinary Essays on Women and Law in India*. Delhi: Kali for Women. pp. 36–60.

Peters, Julia and Andrea Wolper (eds.). 1995. *Women's Rights, Human Rights*. London: Routledge.

Rao, Usha N.J. 1992. 'Gaps in Definitions and Analysis: A Sociological Perspective.' *In* K. Saradamoni (ed.) *Finding the Household, Conceptual and Methodological Issues*. Delhi: Sage Publications. pp. 31–74.

Saradamoni, K. (ed.). 1992. *Finding the Household. Conceptual and Methodological Issues*. Delhi: Sage Publications.

Shah, A.M. 1973. *The Household Dimension of the Family in India*. Delhi: Orient Longman Ltd.

—. 1998. *The Family in India. Critical Essays*. Delhi: Orient Longman Ltd.

Singh, K.S. 1988. 'Tribal Women: An Anthropological Perspective.' *In* J.P. Singh, N. Vyas and R.S. Mann (eds.) *Tribal Women and Development*. Jaipur: Rawat Publications. pp. 31–74.

Walby, Sylvia. 1990. *Theorizing Patriarchy*. Oxford and Cambridge: Blackwell Publishers.

Xaxa, Virginius. 2004. 'Women and Gender in the Study of Tribes in India'. *Indian Journal of Gender Studies*, Vol. 11, No. 3, pp. 345–67.

11

Customary Practices and Human Rights of Tribal Women

ANJANA

Customary Practices: Is it a Source of Patriarchal and Patrilineal Power?

Customary practices still determine the life and choices of majority of tribal women in India and elsewhere. These practices operate as para-legal force; they may provide liberatory space to tribal women in many contexts but they also subordinate and subject them to the existing patrilineal and patriarchal social arrangements. Feminist scholars like Hasan (1994) have argued how in the vote bank politics in India, the state negotiates with the community and legitimizes those customary practices which may prove detrimental to the interest of women. Customary practices inhere power that not only determines how a person should behave and conduct in everyday life but they also determine how people as collectivity perceive and judge the events and conducts of individual and groups. It reminds Lukes' (1974) concept of power where he explicates that power is exercised not by individuals, but also by "socially structured and culturally patterned behaviour of groups and practices of institutions" and hence the individuals (read gendered) "operate within substantially determined limits". Bourdieu's (1977) concept of doxa is also worth noting here. Doxa comprises those ideologies and practices, which are accepted as natural and self-evident part of social order, which goes without saying and not opened to questioning or contestation – the un-discussed, unnamed, admitted without argument or scrutiny. A good deal of what is justified in the name of 'tradition' would fall in this category.

As has already been said above that all customary practices are not detrimental to the interest of women, many feminist writings have also lamented the erasure of customary practices during colonial and post-colonial transition, mostly initiated through state interventions (see Agarwal, 1994). The role of state has always been disfavouring women's interest in this context. While state initiated processes have led to the erosion of 'progressive' elements of tribal customs, they have reinforced the retrograde elements of a given custom.

Empirical Illustrations

Against the above backdrop, it becomes imperative to make certain empirical illustrations of the customary practices in tribal societies. Based on secondary sources, some of the patrilineal and matrilineal tribal communities have been taken for comparison. The societies which have been selected for analysis are Garo, Khasis, Todas of Nilgiri and Ho women of Singbhum.

Pre-colonial Phase

Since the emphasis is on diachronic analysis, the customary practices of the above societies will be dealt with in traditional set-up, i.e., before the penetration of colonial economy and administration. The basic focus of inquiry would be to see the relationship between men and women in terms of access to and control over and transmission of property. Secondly, to what extent and in what respect women themselves and their offspring constitute property (see Hirschon, 1984). With the value premise that tribal women everywhere ought to have a rightful place in the customary, changing and changed cultural milieu and their involvement is essential in all programmes of change and development, it is timely that the status of tribal women is assessed as it is or as it was (Singh, Vyas and Mann, 1985).

At the turn of the 20th century the Garo community of north-east India was practising *jhum* (shifting) cultivation with ten-to-thirty-year rotation. Women played a major role in crop production and gathering of forest produce (Agarwal, 1994). Their labour input was greater than that of men, and their knowledge of crop varieties was extensive. They controlled the household's food surplus and any cash they earned from the sale of small items in the village or the weekly market was considered exclusively theirs (ibid). The Garo community at this time had considerable equality in class and gender terms, although there were certain spheres of authority (e.g., jural) which men alone enjoyed. The bride's and groom's families were equal in status and no dowry and brideprice were exchanged (ibid). All property (movables and ancestral house) other than land passes from mother to chosen daughter, usually the youngest. In case of divorce, the husband could depart with his clothing but little else. Men as husbands and matrilineal kinsmen enjoyed considerable rights and control and jural authority was vested in men alone (ibid: 103).

The Khasis had complex system of local administration. Settlements were formed into Khasi 'states' through the voluntary associations of groups of villages headed by hereditary or elected (usually male) chiefs who exercised judicial and executive authority within multi-tiered councils (ibid). The family's ancestral property – land and ancestral house and movables – passed from mother to youngest daughter (the heiress) who was essentially its custodian. In any case men had considerable control over the management of property as brothers and maternal uncles. Both women and men enjoyed considerable sexual freedom before marriage, but post-marital sexual norms were stricter for women than for men. Adultery by women was subject to heavy fine, could lead to divorce and could deprive an heiress of her rights to ancestral property. Men's adulterous behaviour were tolerated; at worse they could lead to divorce (see Nakane, 1967). Although divorce was common among Khasis for any sufficient cause and often without any assignable reason except mutual dislike or want of children, it was more frequent among heiress who also usually initiated it. Non-heiress daughters were usually more dependent on their husbands since they could except only limited help from their maternal *iing* (Agarwal, 1994: 107). The non-heiress daughters' marriage was more stable, whereas heiress's stronger fall back position clearly made them less tolerant of the husband's authority or shortcomings. It is a popular notion that in traditional Khasi community life women had more freedom and rights than men. Nongbri, a Khasi scholar, contests this claims as she writes:

> In Khasi society, the rule that women alone can inherit ancestral property considered as being discriminatory toward men ... I shall try to demonstrate that Khasis ideas and norms regarding kinship and gender roles, which are apparently weighed in favour of women, are not so in fact (1993: 177).

Nongbri explores the aspects of gender discriminatory practices which are integral part of Khasi society. She says that because Khasi physiology stresses the centrality of woman in the process of reproduction, she is also seen as the centre of family circle. She is expected to be fully responsible for nurturance and care of her children. She is repository of family honour. However women are central to Khasi ideology, writes Nongbri (ibid), they need to be protected and guarded by men. The gender ideology and role models of men and women are vividly brought out in their folk dances. The Khasi dance form gives salience to grace and discipline of women. During their festivals women dance in centre of the circle with their eyes downcast in an act of modesty and restraint. Men dance, forming a protective ring around them holding either a sword or weed brush in hand (ibid). The sword symbolizes protection and defence, while administration, guidance and advice are symbolized by weed brush. Hence, the Khasis say, "war and politics for women, property and children for women" (ibid).

This ideology is reflected in the fact that the Khasi women are not allowed to attend traditional village and 'State Durbars' (customary, administrative and judicial councils). Men jealously guard their prerogatives by defining politics as an arena for mature and physically fit persons. Nongbri demonstrates that the kinship norms and ideology are more lenient to men than to women as far as transgressions of rules are concerned. A man's responsibility ends when he terminates the marriage. If he indulges in extra-marital affair or polygynous unions, his behaviour is not only tolerated but occasionally encouraged. If a woman neglects her obligation to her matrilineal household, she may be even deprived of her property, but if her brother fails to meet his obligations, she is expected to take over her duties. Hence, many Khasi women are constantly working and trying to raise resources because in addition to their own duties they have to step in when men fail to fulfil their obligations.

The Todas are a society with pastoral subsistence base. They reside in and around Nilgiri Hills in Tamil Nadu. The conditions of reproduction in Toda society are contained in the exchange relations that they maintain with the other groups in Nilgiris. Hence, the Todas are not comparable to those pastoralists who are self-reproducing system (see Majumdar and Madan, 1994). The Todas have been known for their overtly gender discriminatory practices. The male supremacist ideology gives the conditions of reproduction in Toda society by enabling the men to, on the one hand, to appropriate the children of the women and on the other, to appropriate subsistence goods from other Nilgiri tribes (see Channa, 1990: 109). The Toda conceptual universe clearly divided the world into pure and impure, which are invariably male and female respectively. The Toda economy is based on dairy. All activities and the objects connected with buffaloes fall into the realm of sacred (or pure). Women are excluded from all these activities. Not only herding and pasturing, even the processing of milk products remained the prerogative of men. All the activities related to milk and milk products took place in the back of house which is pure/sacred and into which women are not allowed. All pathways associated with sacred dairies are pure and no woman can walk on them, nor can a woman walk in front of sacred dairy.

The most ritually impure occasion among the Toda is child birth. But, for the continuation of patrilineage by which a Toda has access to means of production – land, water and buffaloes – as well as for demographic reproduction of their society, men must appropriate women's children (see Channa, 1990). There are two important social mechanisms applied by Todas to maintain their demographic balances: polyandry and female infanticide. Among the Todas women have almost no property rights. All resources are jointly held by patrilineage for the benefits of its male descendants alone. Since the Todas are almost entirely dependent on milk of buffalos for subsistence, the number of female buffaloes in the society must be greater than that of human population. Hence, it is necessary to curtail human population. Interrelated to some extent with polyandry is the practice of female infanticide. This results for Toda women in the exclusion from productive activities. Because of extremely limited role of Toda women in productive activities, it is economically viable for a number of husbands to share a wife.

Verghese (1987) has quoted both Berreman and Murdoch who write: "it has been observed that polyandry is related to sex specialization in which women make only an insignificant contribution to subsistence. One can ask here, as to women voluntarily make an insignificant contribution to subsistence or they are forced to do so by customary practices?" Rosaldo (1974: 22) aptly writes: "In many patrilineal ideologies, women are seen as unnecessary or superfluous, yet at the same time vitally important to men: they are needed as wives, as sisters to be exchanged for wives and as procreators who produce workers and heirs for the group. Because they are important, they are powerful, yet theirs is a power opposed to formal norms ... in such situations, culture may elaborate the idea of her pollution a woman's activities are circumscribed by calling them dangerous, by making them something to fear".

The *Adivasis* of Jharkhand – are divided – into two main linguistic groups. The other are tribes who speak the language of Dravidian group. The phenomenon of witch-hunting is much noted and commented upon (see Kelkar and Nathan, 1991). A woman, when without husband and father, has a residual life interest in land. She can dispose of the produce and income from the land as she wants. This life interest of a widow restricts the property rights of male agnates of the deceased husband whose use of this land for accumulation or for consumption has to wait till after the death of the woman.

Witches are almost entirely women that too widows without support of children. Such widows have life interest in land which, after their death, will pass into the hands of male agnates of their husbands. Such women being denounced as witches, and then driven away or killed, would result in the lands immediately passing into the hands of husbands' male agnates. This economic interest has been veiled in mythology which justifies the practice of witch-hunting. The categorization of women and men into witches and witch-finders respectively provides the fertile ground for witch-hunting.

Colonial and Post-colonial

In both mainstream political science and classical Marxism, state action has been explained in terms of state-society interaction. But they have been primarily gender-neutral. Margot Lovett (see Parpart and Staudt, 1989: 23–46) problemetizes class formation in East, Central and Southern Africa during colonial period as gendered processes. The pre-colonial patterns of authority were manipulated and/or invoked by men during colonial period to justify the gendering of rural class formation. In particular, catalyzed by expanding cash-crop production, and with the active co-operation of colonial state, men's supervisory rights over land were increasingly transformed into ownership rights. As land owners, men also received modern agricultural inputs. Under the same conditions, however, women's usufructuary and trusteeship rights in land became increasingly threatened and vulnerable (ibid). Everywhere, the political elite is largely male. For all variations in states—weak or strong, more or less autonomous—one constant remains is that women are *never* central to state power.

All feminist scholars agree that colonialism and capitalism restructured traditional economies in a way which had profound impact on women's economic activities, the nature of sexual division of labour and the kinds of social and political options which remained opened to women (Rapp, 1977). Another important dimension, which is equally important, is to see the contradictory constitutive elements or institutional practices of the state. Constitutional equal rights may co-exist with institutionalized male privilege; policies to promote female emancipation alongside those fostering female dependency (Moore, 1988). Western feminists have long argued that state tends to promote a particular 'family' household structure – the male wage earner with the dependent wife and children. These policies are not necessarily designed with the intention of oppressing and discriminating against women, but according to prevailing notions, assumptions and ideologies about the role of women, the nature of family and proper relations between men and women. The end result is that the state policies may be highly contradictory (ibid).

It is against this backdrop that the impact of colonial policies on some of these tribal communities in India needs to be examined from (tribal) women's perspectives. To begin with the Garos, it appears that the establishment of control over Garo Hills in the second half of 19th century led to substantial changes in economic and social fabric which were carried further by post-independence policies (Agrawal, 1994). Many of these changes adversely affected the community in general and women in particular. Bina Agarwal (ibid) shows as to how wet cultivation was superimposed by colonial administration culminating in inter-and intra-village differentiation and also there was a significant change in gender division of labour. Wet cultivation required substantial changes in agricultural techniques; land preparation for wet rice needs more care than for *jhum* rice since ploughing and levelling are often necessary, requiring new skills and draft animals. Its harvesting requires sickle and threshing has to be done with cattle etc. Agarwal makes very significant point here. She (ibid: 158) says, "in themselves these changes need not reduce women's contributions to production, but they have tended to do so since the new skills are taught mainly to men".

The British, and after independence the state government, began to grant *pattas* (titles) to individuals and accelerated the shift to settled cultivation and privatization. The *pattas* were typically granted in male names (ibid: 159). Parents want to bequeath some private land to sons, since sons became familiar with wet rice cultivation techniques by working with fathers in their fields. The spread of Christianity, while associated with the advance of education for both sexes, had also led to decline of customary, communal and ritual practices—women's sexual freedom has declined (ibid). To Agarwal, the history of north-eastern matrilineal tribes strikingly illustrates how the shift from land as a communal resource to land under individual possession has been associated not only with well-recognized processes of class differentiation but with equally critical gender differentiation among the peasantry.

Kishwar (1987), writing about Ho women of Singhbhum argues that most attempts at tribal development have essentially meant furthering their subjection and pushing tribal society into a completely male dominated and hierarchical mould. The emulation of Hindu peasant norms has led to the erosion of features which had positive consequences for women (ibid). As it is taboo for women to plough, if there is no male member in the family a woman has to hire a male for this work. While a woman cannot meet her survival need without male help her labour cannot be substituted by hired help. Ho women cannot sale of mortgage a piece of land as it is not in their name.

Kelkar and Nathan (1991) delve into the patriarchal discourses which inform the political movements like Santhal rebellion during British period and more recent Jharkhand organizations. The discourse at a later stage culminated into what is called the house-wifization process. Like the Christian churches, the JMM (Jharkhand Mukti Morcha) took up a programme of teaching domestic craft to women such as cookery, stitching, embroidery etc. (ibid). In the name of preventing the sexual and moral corruption of tribal women by non-tribal men, women either divorced or separated, working in collieries or engaged in petty trade, were first warned that they should marry. If they refused to obey, they were beaten up and even married off to some, chosen by caders and sent away from their homes and worksites to distant areas where their 'new' husbands resided. This is a novel form of devaluing women under the guise of enforcing sexual morality and has given rise to corrupt practices.

Conclusion

From the perspectives of tribal women customary practices combines both liberatory elements and entitlements but they also contain gender discriminatory practices alongside. Moreover, in modifying the customary practices, the colonial and post-colonial state work not in the interest of women but they are mostly guided by political expediencies and their own conscious, unconscious ethnocentric assumptions. A large number of feminist writings have brought to light how state interacts with the community and who speaks in the name of the community. Since women are never central to the power and state processes, the sate, by and large, represents patriarchal interest. In codifying and preserving local culture they negotiate with the elite men of community and not the women. This has always worked at the detriment of women. While the state may modify certain women-friendly customs and reinforce and legitimize gender discriminatory practices. But here, we cannot dispense with the state altogether but the women's group need to intervene and participate in this rhetoric of cultural preservation and state and community initiated change.

References

Agarwal, Bina. 1994. *A Field of One's Own: Gender and Land Rights in South Asia.* Cambridge: Cambridge University Press.

Bourdieu, Pierre. 1977. *Outline of a Theory of Practice.* Trans. R. Nice. Cambridge: Cambridge University Press.

Channa, Subhadra. 1990. 'Ideology, Production and Re-production: Pre-capitalist Social Formation among the Toda'. *Eastern Anthropologists.* 43, 1 pp. 100–22.

Hasan, Joya (ed.). 1994. *Forging Identity: Gender, Communities and State.* New Delhi: Kali for Women.

Hirschon, Renee (ed.). *Women and Property: Women as Property.* London: Croom Helm.

Kelkar, G. and D. Nathan. 1991. *Gender and Tribe: Women, Land and Forests in Jharkhand.* New Delhi: Kali for Women.

Lukes, S. 1974. *Power: A Radical View.* London: Macmillan.

Majumdar, D.N. and T.N. Madan. 1994. *Social Anthropology.* Delhi: Mayoor Paperbacks.

Moore, Henrietta L. 1988. *Feminism and Anthropology.* Cambridge: Polity Press.

Nakane, C. 1967. *Garo and Khasi: A Comparative Study in Matrilineal System.* Paris: Mouton.

Nongbri, Tiplut. 1993. 'Gender and Khasi Family Structure'. *In* Patricia Uberoi (ed.), *Family, Marriage and Kinship in India.* New Delhi: Oxford University Press.

Parpart, Jane l. and Staudt, K.A. (eds.). 1989. *Women and State in Africa.* Boulder: Lynne Reinner Publishers.

Rapp, Rayana. 1977. 'Gender and Class: An Archaeology of Knowledge Concerning the Origin of State'. *Dialectical Anthropology.* Vol. 2.

Rosaldo, Michelle Z. 1980. 'The Use and Abuse of Anthropology: Reflexions on feminism and Cross-cultural Understanding'. *Signs.* Vol. 5, no. 3 pp. 389–427.

Singh, J.P., N.N. Vyas and R.S. Mann (eds.). 1985. *Tribal Women and Development.* Udaipur: The MLV Tribal Research Institute.

Verghese,. I. 1987. 'Polyandry in Kota Society: An Appraisal'. *In* M.N. Raha (ed.) *Polyandry in India.* Delhi: Gyan Publishing House.

12

Tribal Women Health Issues in Human Rights Perspective

Some Insights from Gujarat

RATNAWALI AND SUDARSHAN IYENGAR

The situation with respect to women's health in India is not satisfactory. Health-related statistics suggest that health status in the country is not encouraging, although the trend reflects some improvement (Visaria and Ramachandran, 1999; Mahadevan et al., 2000; Ramasubban and Jejeebhoy, 2000; Visaria et al., 2004). The position of Gujarat state with respect to human development indicators including health is not good (Duggal, 2005; Hirway and Mahadevia, 2005). Even the economic development is not spread evenly. It is necessary therefore to examine region-specific situation in Gujarat. Women's health has been one of the main concerns reflected in human development debate in Gujarat (Hirway and Mahadevia, 2005). In this paper, an attempt is made to review the issues related to tribal women's reproductive health. It is understood that the state has not done well and there is a trend to rely more on the private initiatives and market forces even for basic service provisions. Under, the changing circumstances, it is being argued that unless one views the health issues in the context of human rights, the pressure on state may disappear almost completely and the public systems may collapse.

Human Rights Perspective in Health and Health Status in India and Gujarat

The sufferings and miseries of Second World War exposed human population to the inherent danger of barbarism and savageries inflicted by war and inter-state or intra-state conflicts. Human dignity was at lower ebb. The turmoil eventually led to some sane thinking and ultimately manifested in the Universal Declaration of Human Rights in 1948 under the aegis of United Nations. These rights are guaranteed to every human being as essential basic rights that one attains by being a member of the human fraternity. It confers upon a woman civil, political, economic, social and cultural rights. Of course, it is applicable to a nation ratifying it. Article 25 of the Universal Declaration of Human Rights states the following in its two sub-clauses:

(1) Everyone has the right to a standard of living adequate for the health and well-being of himself and of his family, including food, clothing, housing and medical care and necessary social services, and the right to security in the event of unemployment, sickness, disability, widowhood or other lack of livelihood in circumstances beyond his control.

(2) Motherhood and childhood are entitled to special care and assistance. All children, whether born in or out of wedlock, shall enjoy the same social protection.

However, right to health took back seat in the so-called greater rights of civil and political categories. Need of the people and promotion of their right to health was actively promoted only after the Alma Ata declaration in 1978. It defined health as complete well-being in the context of the environment, i.e., socio-economic and political, as well as within the ambit of development. The declaration advocated people's participation in planning and implementation of health services. Though the declaration brought the importance of health in the international arena, special attention to women for her additional responsibility in child bearing was not given. Thus women, besides suffering from other abuses that the men suffered also, suffered on sexual and reproductive health issues. Realizing the misery, the Convention on the Elimination of All Forms of Discrimination

Against Women (CEDAW) specified reproductive rights of women under Articles 10(h), 12(1), 14.2(c), and Article 16(1) (Human Rights Watch, 1998). Article 16(1) of CEDAW provides: "State parties shall take all appropriate measures to ... ensure on a basis of equality of men and women ... the same rights to decide freely and responsibly on the number and spacing of their children and to have access to the information, education and means to enable them to exercise their rights" (Human Rights Watch, 1998).

Despite these safeguards and rights established in the international conventions and declarations, women's exploitation continues and they are denied basic rights that are necessary for their survival during child bearing. Their subordinate status is reinforced by the cultural practices and legal bindings. Seldom are they seen as a person with physical integrity and personal autonomy but are regarded more as an object of family and community honour in most of the countries in the world. The discontent and growing concern towards their rights led to their recognition worldwide by the governments at the World Conference on Human Rights in Vienna in 1993 where it got accepted as "an inalienable, integral and indivisible part of universal human rights" (Human Rights Watch, 1998). However, notwithstanding this recognition, there remains a large gap between government rhetoric and reality where their rights are frequently trampled over by the state leaving them vulnerable to the frequent abuses at the domestic front, employment, civil and state conflicts and during detention in the legal police custody of the governments.

At the International Conference on Population and Development (ICPD) in Cairo in 1994, governments recognized that "advancing gender equality and equity and the empowerment of women, and the elimination of all kinds of violence against women, and ensuring women's ability to control their own fertility, are cornerstones of population and development-related programmes" (Human Rights Watch, 1998). It thus brought reproductive health within the ambit of human rights and protected women from the state that too abuses women's health rights by implementing policies that regulate women's sexual and reproductive decision-making to suit its population control strategies. The ICPD recognized reproductive health right as:

1. A satisfying and safe sex life free from the fear of disease and, coercion and violence.
2. The right to be informed and have access to effective, affordable and acceptable methods of family planning of their choice on the one hand and access to infertility services on the other.
3. The ability to go safely through pregnancy and child birth and have the best chance of having a healthy infant and the right of access to appropriate health care services.
4. Access to safe and affordable abortion facility.
5. Access to services for the prevention and care of sexual and reproductive health problems, both gynaecological and obstetrics, in a culturally sensitive manner.
6. The right of all, including women, men and married and unmarried adolescents, to information and services including counselling, whether on contraception, pregnancy, diseases or the complications of coerced sex, and the freedom to make decisions on the basis of this information.

India being a signatory to all these international declarations has responsibility to follow the commitments in letter and spirit. The National Population Policy, 2000 acknowledges women's health care in rights perspective. It is expected that the health programmes run by the central and the state governments also in spirit recognize the women health issues in human rights perspective. Evidence about this should get reflected eventually in the health status indicators worked out periodically by national and international organizations. It is more than a decade when ICPD laid down clearly the women's rights with respect to health. The Human Development Report, 2004 has published statistics on various indicators related to women's health. We present below the data on some important indicators and compared them with the neighbouring countries, including China:

Table 1 reflects that with regard to women and child health, India does not present a picture better than its neighbours. It is particularly worse than its most neighbours in IMR, MMR, and infants with low birth weight. China and Sri Lanka have registered

Table 1

Important Women's Health Indicators in India and Neighbouring Countries as per HDR, 2004

Countries	*GDI Rank*	*LE at birth Female*	*IMR 2002*	*MMR 2000*	*Birth Attd. %*	*Infant with LBW %*	*Under nourished Popu. 1999 to 2001%*	*CPR %*	*Health Expenditure % of GDP 2001*		
									Public	Private	Total
India	103	64.4	67	540	43	30	21	48	0.9	4.2	5.1
Nepal	116	59.4	66	740	11	21	17	39	1.5	3.6	5.1
Bangladesh	110	61.5	51	380	12	30	32	54	1.6	2.0	3.6
Pakistan	120	60.7	83	500	20	19	19	28	1.0	3.0	4.0
Shri Lanka	73	75.8	17	92	97	22	25	N.A.	1.8	1.9	3.7
China	71	73.2	31	56	76	6	11	84	2.0	3.4	5.4
Developing Countries	N.A.	N.A	61	N.A.	55	N.A.	N.A.	N.A.	N.A.	N.A.	N.A.
World	N.A.	N.A	56	N.A.	58	N.A.	17	N.A.	N.A.	N.A.	N.A.

N.A. Not Available.

GDI = Gender-related Development Index; LEB = Life Expectancy at Birth (2000 to 05); IMR = Infant Mortality Rate 2002; MMR = Maternal Mortality Rate (per 100,000 live births) 2000; Birth Attd. Birth Attended by Skilled Health Worker 1995 to 2002; LBW = Low Birth Weight 1998 to 2002; CPR = Contraceptive Prevalence Rate 1995 to 2002.

Source: Human Development Report 2004.

better health status in comparison to India in most of the parameters that we have taken into consideration. Even the RCH programme initiated by the government well before 1997 does not seem to have made much impact on the health status of women. India recorded a poor public expenditure on health, which again is lowest among its neighbours. Even this expenditure does not seem to be spent well on poor. Its 60 of health care spending is availed by high and middle income groups in urban sector (Kamath, 2004). The World Bank Report on Health Policy Research in South Asia shows that the disparity in rural-urban health beneficiaries is disquieting. The per capita health benefit is at least four times greater in urban area compared with rural area (*Indian Economic Review,* 2004). The inequalities in utilization of subsidies granted to this sector can be gauged by the fact that the richest 20 per cent capture about 31 per cent of the subsidies meant for the poor, while 20 per cent of the poorest use only 10 per cent of the same. Declining utilization of public health care infrastructure itself is a testimony to the sorrow state of affairs.

Health being a concurrent subject the states too own responsibilities to deliver health services as per the requirement of population. However, differential status of health among the states appears to suggest that the states are not doing better as expected. Duggal (2005) shows that among the western states in India, Gujarat, being one of the most developed states of India and a state with well-established health care infrastructure, continues to report lower levels of health indicators. The data presented in Table 2 reinforces the above facts.

In general, it can be said that Gujarat has better health status compared with the country as a whole. It is well served in term of established infrastructure. On an average, there is one medical institution serving to a population of 29,045. Further, health facilities are located more in rural areas (77.6) than in urban areas (22.4). Tribal districts in the state seem to be better provided in terms of availability of health centres. About 82 per cent of the facilities are located in the rural areas (Government of Gujarat 2002). However, utilization of services as reflected from indoor and outdoor patients appear to be substantially low in the tribal district as a whole. It, therefore, refers to the fact that these

Table 2

Health Indicators for Western and Central States in India

States	*IMR 98–99*	*Life expectancy at birth*	*% pregnant women receiving full ANC*	*% children fully immunized*	*% of institutional deliveries*	*Percentage of women with BMI below 18.5 kg per meter square*	*% children with weight by height below – 2 S.D.*
Gujarat	62.6	61.4	25	53.0	46.3	37.0	16.2
Madhya Pradesh	86.1	55.2	10.9	22.4	20.1	38.2	19.8
Maharashtra	43.7	65.2	31	78.6	52.6	20.2	21.2
Rajasthan	80.4	59.5	8.3	17.3	21.5	36.1	11.7
India	67.6	60.7	20	74.0	33.36	35.8	15.5

Source: Duggal, 2005.

facilities are little utilized by the tribals though they physically exist in the tribal locations. The situation calls for attention to look into the quality of services offered by these institutions. Health indicators for tribal population confirm this impression. Table 3 below contains some health profile indicators for tribal women in Gujarat:

Table 3

Reproductive Health Indicators among Tribal Women

Health Indicator	*Value 1998–99*
Percentage of women having at least one ANC	77.8
Immunized with TT (%)	73.0
Iron folic tablets to pregnant women (%)	69.4(86.9)*
Institutional delivery	28.8
Use of contraceptive among currently married women any method (%)	57.1

*figures in bracket indicate percentage compliance.

Source: NFHS 1998–99, Gujarat Report.

It may be observed that among tribal women in Gujarat, ANC check up is largely limited to one visit. Most of the deliveries take place at home only. TT immunization is not cent per cent (Iyengar and Ratnawali, 2004). In this backdrop, we now look at what women in the tribal areas had to say on their reproductive health problems.

Tribal Women's Perception of their Reproductive Health Problems

At the outset, it must be recognized that the tribal societies, although relatively well integrated with the mainstream in respect to economic activities, have definite cultural heritage. This difference manifests in their beliefs, perceptions and practices in many areas, including health. It is known that tribal settlements have been generally away from the non-tribal settlements and have remained isolated in terms of socio-cultural practices. Physical distances have also been a formidable obstacle in reaching the state sponsored services to remotely settled people – be it in the sub-sectors of health, education or public distribution systems. The tribal societies have therefore evolved their own survival strategies and coping mechanisms in crisis and this includes health sector as well. After independence, in the absence of imaginative designs of health services, lack of committed staff in the health and education sector, genuine resource constraints and lack of effective monitoring and administration, the state sponsored services have hardly reached the tribal people. Thus, even after more than sixty years of independence, many of the tribal areas suffered from lack of access to good and reliable health services. Tribal women, although having relatively better social status than many mainstream social strata, suffered particularly with respect to the reproductive health-related problems.

Introduction of RCH programme has effected some change in the service providing environment. The RCH programme has evolved out of the experiences in planning and implementing many specific programmes such as family planning, safe motherhood and others (for details, refer Visaria and Ramachandran, 2000). Along with the RCH programme, the Bhuria Committee, which was set up to take a comprehensive look at the tribal development, also helped by way of recommending better health infrastructure. We thought that it might be useful to assess the situation in tribal areas and understand what the tribal women think and understand about the availability, accessibility and utilization of health services. The study has been less ambitious in the sense that we have selected only two talukas (blocks) in a tribal district – Valsad – and conducted about a dozen focus group discussions and a few in-depth interviews with women and service providers (for details on methodology, refer Iyengar and Ratnawali, 2004). The focus group discussions (FGDs) with women revealed that they suffer from a number of reproductive health problems. These problems and their perceptions about them are presented here briefly, which also contextualize the health-seeking behaviour among them.

Dysmenorrhoea and leucorrhoea are identified as most prevalent problems, however, these are perceived as normal and generally no medical intervention is sought. Less bleeding accompanied with abdominal pain too is reported as a problem and is attributed to accumulation of blood clots that restricts free flow of blood.

Pregnancy and delivery, though are perceived as vulnerable periods, some of the frequently met problems like odema, night blindness, abdominal pain, bleeding and watery discharge are not taken seriously. Nor do they seek treatment for the same as they are considered routine problems and would go with the birth of child. Deliveries are handled by Dhais (traditional birth attendant) who by and large are trained. Prolonged pain, heavy bleeding, breech child and discharge of fluid long before the birth of baby (sukhi suvavad) are some of the problems which are often faced during delivery. Among them sukhi suvavad and protrusion of uterus along with baby (it is their perception but medically it may be residual part of placenta or some uterine membrane) are perceived serious as these require intervention mostly of the expertise of Dhais. Besides, delay in expelling placenta after the birth of child or early descend of placenta before delivery of the baby, still birth and delay in delivery leading to death of child and at times mother, are some of the problems which are encountered at the time of delivery. No wonder anxieties regarding safe delivery predominates their reproductive health problems. Even after delivery, problems like back pain and weakness are commonly experienced and are taken casually. These are left to be cured in gradual process and little attention is paid towards their treatment. Prolonged bleeding, fits and abdominal pain are taken with little sincerity and are preferred to be treated either by Bhagat's[1] medicine or home remedy. Breast abscess too seldom gets treated by doctor unless it goes beyond remedial measures of their own and that of Bhagat's. It is generally believed that formal medicines are 'hot'[2] in constituent and they can dry lactation. Neonatal problems like cough, cold, fever, sepsis in umbilicus are also frequently reported and are treated at home by herbs and are later taken to doctor if situation deteriorates.

Infertility significantly finds mention as one of the problems faced by women in most of the villages. Its treatment is first sought by Bhagat as infertility is believed to be brought by evil effect of 'Bhamra' (pattern of hair twirls at the back of head of the child and at the back of the woman). It is treated by branding called 'Daam'. Sometimes slits are made in the abdomen of the woman and are filled with herbs to cure the problem. Women sometimes frequently undertake 'Daam' to beget child in order to save their marriage as divorce in such cases are accepted norm. In desperation she frequents between medical doctor and Bhagat as well. Infertility is normally perceived as women-specific disorder, hence their husbands generally do not seek treatment or visit doctor for the same. Some of the commonly held perceptions identified as reasons that cause obstruction in normal conception are heat in womb, irregular menses and less bleeding during menstruations. Hence, cleansing of uterus by medical practitioner or herbal medicines is relied upon for its treatment.

Almost at every FGD, most of the women who had suffered miscarriage or had experienced spontaneous abortion, who declared it to be a commonly occurring problem and precaution is taken by simply avoiding hot food. Evil spirits are believed to be the cause behind such phenomena. Sometimes 'Bhamra' is also regarded as a cause of bringing evil effect upon women's foetus leading to miscarriage. Diarrhoea, weakness and excess bleeding are also some of the causes which according to women lead to loss of pregnancy. Hot constitution of body and hot food are also identified as factors responsible for the situation. Tablets and injections too are avoided as they are perceived to be hot, and rituals are observed to correct the disorder. Induced abortion did not find mention in the FGDs unless specifically asked. Even then it was little bit discussed and generally women pleaded ignorance regarding its practices. However, its prevalence in the community is not denied in case of pregnancy outside marriage or in unwed women. It was revealed in the in-depth interview that abortion facility is availed at nearby village by a knowledgeable woman or at distant government facility for the sake of privacy. Private facilities are explored for better service and for privacy though they are expensive. Some of the abortificient according to them are papaya, herbal concoction, hot fomentation or hot tea though proper medical assistance is considered the safest way. Married women mostly prefer to continue with their pregnancy even if it is unwanted.

Spacing methods as means to limit family size are by and large unknown to women. The only option known to them is sterilization and is practised widely. Even where women had heard about these methods, they had not seen nor had used them personally. Assistance of ANM for sterilization is easily available to them, hence they prefer opting for the same. Male sterilization is not preferred as it is believed to cause weakness and gradual illness in man. In some villages where women had come across these reversible methods, oral pills are preferred over Copper-T as the latter is believed to cause discomfort and pain. Bleeding is also reported as a consequence of inserting Copper-T. However oral pills too are not thought as good option, as it has to be taken with regularly.

Behavioural Attitude Towards Health Care

Tribals, having belief in soul and spirit, associate most of the health disorders with them. Hence, services of Bhagat (religious head and medicine man) are sought first in most cases of illness. Even though they realize the importance of modern medicine, their first approach to Bhagat is common. Tribal society perceives them as wise and knowledgeable to handle spiritual and physical cause of illness. Women too seek their help in most of their reproductive health problems. His accessibility comes handy to them, as he lives within the village, or in neighbouring villages. Considering tribal settlement pattern in interior and remote places, he is the only person easily accessible to provide medical relief. Though reliance on modern system has risen considerably, Bhagat continues to play an important role in providing health services. He is trusted with the treatment for minor to critical illnesses. His medicines are sought for leucorrhoea, menstrual disorders, infertility and spontaneous abortion. In case of infertility and spontaneous abortions, herbal medicines or rituals are also resorted to. Women seek his services even to get relief from prolonged labour pain and in case of STDs. Sometimes effectiveness of Bhagat's treatment is also acknowledged over effect of modern medicine when later takes time in manifestation.

For pregnancy and delivery services Dhais are most relied upon. Her experiences and skills in managing deliveries are acknowledged by all women. During pregnancy too her advices are valued and her assessment regarding duration of pregnancy and prospective delivery dates are taken with seriousness. She assesses complications and keep women informed about the same. It helps people to make up their mind to be prepared for institutional delivery at the time of crisis. Her closeness with community and easy accessibility at the hour of need, enhances her role in providing specialized services in the matter of pregnancy and child birth. Dais are further relied for their perseverance and insistence to normal delivery rather than surgical interventions adopted by doctors.

Thus formal health service systems find little place in their health seeking behaviour. Limited access to these services has failed to restore their faith in them. Antenatal care check-up is neither done fully nor is valued by them. Irregularity of ANM is one of their major concerns. However, medicines for weakness, excess bleeding during menstruation, irregular menses and leucorrhoea are some of the problems for which medicines from ANM are sought if she is accessible. She is also known for her immunization services in general and polio vaccination in particular. Her irregular visit to remote village makes women less dependent upon her. Post-delivery services too are virtually non-existent in far-flung areas. Hence, illnesses of infants and mother are first treated at village level and doctors are contacted only when situation deteriorates. It sometimes results in the death of new born and complications for mother. Excessive bleeding or delayed birth, breech births, eclampsia and discharge of water much before delivery are some of the problems when women are taken to hospital as Primary Health Centre (PHC) lacks adequate expertise and infrastructure in dealing with such cases. Dharampur, Valsad, Vapi, Pardi, Peth and Silvasa are some of the places which are accessed by women depending upon the distance from their villages. It sometimes causes delay and foster sufferings to the women.

Adoption of contraceptives is negligible among women. It is generally because of their ignorance. Though oral pills are provided by ANMs but where their services are regular, its acceptance has not picked up. Sterilization is most easily available and is widely adopted. ANMs facilitate this service by taking them to the centres and accompany them back to their villages. These operations are conducted at Community Health Centre (CHC) or public hospitals in Dharampur or in Valsad.

Women's Perceptions about Formal Health Services

Women in general expressed their desire to have accessibility to health services particularly during crises. In all interviews, delivery, spontaneous abortion and infertility appeared to be most critical to them and necessity and availability of qualified doctor was felt most. Preference for lady doctor was obvious. However, presence of a qualified doctor to meet emergency requirement is vociferously expressed, particularly during monsoon when these villages loose access to road. ANM's visits to villages were reported to be poor. In some of the villages they had not even seen ANM. In some, it was reported that she came for immunizing children only. But where she resides at village women acknowledged her work and expressed satisfaction.

PHC, in the opinion of women, provides only limited services with regard to their reproductive health problems. It attends to the problems related to menstruation, leucorrhoea, skin diseases, breast abscess, and other general ailments. Complete ANC check-up seems to be availed mainly by the women living near these services. It was opined that doctors are present in health centres but women in general were not satisfied with medical investigations carried out there. Dispensing of medicine is moderate, hence, some drugs have to be purchased from outside. One of their concerns was that doctors provide only tablets, which are less effective, whereas injections were more effective and were not administered. It was felt that it was futile to visit PHC as most of the cases were referred to other big hospitals. Behaviour of the staff and doctors in PHC was not always good. Complaint was also made against a doctor at a CHC who did not pay adequate attention to patients. Occurrence of such behaviour also deterred women from seeking services in the formal government sector. One such incidence was also reported when a woman from Lavkar village went to Kaprada CHC to have TL operation. When the nurse came to know that she had been enrolled at Lavkar PHC, the woman was not treated well and even denied the iron tablets. However, on the next day, she was offered medicine but she refused it out of anger. Such incidents erode women's faith in getting good treatment in the government set-up. Distances and lack of transportation facilities were also highlighted as the reasons that prohibited women from utilizing existing government health facilities.

Formal Health Infrastructure in Villages

In the backdrop of problems and perceptions of women, the existing state of affair in the formal health services was probed by interviewing the service providers at these centres and observing the physical state of health centres. The government has a provision of one PHC for a population of 20,000 and one sub-centre for a population of 3,000 in tribal areas. However, it was found that these standards were not strictly adhered to. Sub-centres at most of the places did not have their own building. They were either run from Aanganwadi or from primary schools. At a few places the premise was rented. Amenities like water and electricity were lacking in most places. Absence of a bed or an examination table was common. PHCs and CHCs though have their own buildings, their maintenance was very poor. In monsoon the ceiling and walls leaked and dripped. Shortage of water, especially during summer, makes it difficult to maintain proper hygiene and use of toilet. Even labour room and operation theatre lack upkeep and proper sterilization. A CHC did not have required number of beds. Indoor patients were found on floor. Doctors at CHC and PHC expressed their concern for lack of modern apparatus and instruments. In their view, they would have discarded the worn out instruments had they been in private practice. Laboratory of these institutions too carried out only preliminary investigation for haemoglobin, malaria, tuberculosis, and urine albumen. However, facility of refrigeration for vaccines and drugs were there. To counter the power failure generators are also provided. Ambulances were also utilized as mobile dispensary vehicle at the time of outbreak of diarrhoea, dysentery and leptospirosis during monsoon. Drivers at some places were not in regular appointment. Thus, the use of ambulance as mobile van defeated the purpose of carrying patients in emergency. Drug situation at PHC was moderate except that some antibiotics and ORS during monsoon were in short supply. The actual number of health functionaries was less than sanctioned positions.

Perceptions and Provisions of Services by Service Providers

We interviewed selected gynaecologists, medical officers and female health workers in order to get insights into their perceptions and services offered by them at various levels in the study area. The ANMs are the grassroots service providers. They are expected to stay at their respective sub-centre but most of them commute daily to their field area. Though they acknowledge that it limits their scope to work and they are not able to cover the entire field area in a month. Lack of full strength often leads to multiple responsibilities and hence it becomes difficult to attend to their duties in the assigned villages. At times the additional duty that they have to carry on by taking up duty at the PHC makes it difficult discharge the assigned duties at the village level. ANMs in antenatal check-up carry out abdominal examination but are not always able to weight and check blood pressure, as equipments are not available to them. The ANMs were overstressed with work. Their main bottleneck in covering entire area was reliable transportation. In such situations it was difficult to visit far off places and provide the required services. Apart from these, maintenance of seven registers, meetings with Aanganwadi workers, Dhais and women left them with no time to accomplishing the main duty assigned to them.

The Medical Officers (MOs) at the PHCs in the study area did not reside there due to improper upkeep of the quarters and problems of water and electricity. Most of them commute daily to their PHCs. MOs reportedly provided immunization, ANC check-ups, family planning and diagnosis of disorders like uterus prolepses, fibroids and RTI-related problems. In ANC check-ups, besides abdominal examination, blood pressure, weight and haemoglobin were also tested. Anaemia was very common among pregnant women and iron tablets were provided to them. In their view, nearly 60 per cent of women completed course of iron folic acid intake. Deliveries were conducted at home as PHCs lacked in facility. The MOs in PHCs referred all surgery cases to other higher public hospitals. Doctors maintained that women felt shy in getting themselves examined by male doctors. Most of the cases pertained to backache, pains in joints, abdominal pain and problems related with menses and leucorrhoea. In the absence of adequate laboratory testing facilities diagnosis of RTI/STI was clinical. However, the number was very low. Shortage of medicine was experienced mostly during monsoon when the cases of diarrhoea, vomiting and fever were reported in large numbers. Though they acknowledged that ANMs worked under constrains, they believed that methodical and dedicated approach of ANM could bring about changes for better. PHCs could be utilized better if proper links to interiors through road and transportation facilities were established.

Valsad Civil Hospital deals with a number of cases referred by PHC and CHC. It has one gynaecologist and is flooded with a variety of surgical and non-surgical complaints though it has only eighteen beds under gynaecology ward. Shortage of personnel was most felt but the hospital had other infrastructural facilities better placed. According to the gynaecologist, for more than a decade, the hospital was largely utilized by the underprivileged tribal and rural womenfolk who could not afford private treatment for the specialized services offered by the hospital. He also held that grassroots workers like ANMs and health workers have been given enormous responsibilities, which in his view reduced their efficiency. He was also concerned about limited training capabilities of trainers and little practical exposure given to ANMs, which rendered them less equipped in dealing with complicated cases.

Assessment of Health Situation and Analysis in the Human Rights Perspective

It is fairly clear from the above that the state has been successful in a limited way in providing health services to fulfil the reproductive health needs of the tribal women. Reproductive health services situation in the tribal areas may be summarized as follows:

1. Tribal women still consider Bhagat as their first health service provider. Though he enjoys this status as part of their tradition, it is also true that non-availability of reliable and credible services also leave women with less option and hence they approach the traditional healer.
2. Due to lack of regular and reliable formal services, most of the problem during pregnancy and post-delivery like night blindness, abdominal pain, bodyache, blood spotting and weakness are internalized as normal associated with these phases of life.
3. The most vulnerable period of pregnancy and delivery is largely uncared and women have little option other than traditional birth attendant (Dhai) trained or untrained. Irregular visits of ANMs also render women to seek services from Dhai till situation turns complicated.
4. ANMs are basically known for immunization work. Though they claim to provide ANC services, women do not acknowledge it. Similarly, post-partum check-up, which is a must within 48 hours of delivery, is not fully provided to women in all villages other than the village in which the ANM happens to live. ANMs tend to collect information from Dhais for the purpose of reporting their work.
5. Women are not fully aware of contraceptive measures to space their pregnancies. Thus, frequent pregnancies expose them to further morbidity, which adversely affects their health, particularly in the light of general anaemia prevailing among them.
6. Sterilization is the only effective option available to them, including women in very young age group of below 30 years. Prompt service of sterilization in particular reflects the government's continued emphasis on family planning.
7. Treatment for spontaneous abortion and infertility are sought from Bhagat. Even if visit to PHC is made, males avoid accompanying, as problem is believed to be women-specific and divorce can be given on this basis. Visit to Bhagat is

made in order to have baby by undergoing successive branding (Daam). This exposes women to serious infections.

8. Although women are reluctant to report RTI and STD-related problems to formal service providers, the PHC-level facilities are not fully equipped for pathological examinations. PHCs in most of the places have male doctors to whom women avoid getting examined, particularly the younger ones. Specialized service of gynaecologist is not available in all CHCs.
9. Lack of information and availability of MTP services at PHC level make women to carry unwanted pregnancies to full term in many cases.
10. Poor service provisions at public hospitals push women either to seek care at private facility or to suffer morbidity.

It is clear from the above that as far as RCH services are concerned, women are not getting adequate treatment from the formal public service system. Even the grassroots workers of these services do not always stay at the village headquarters. As a result, they are not able to make necessary visits and attend to most of the reproductive health needs of these women. The state apparatus, therefore, seems to be negligent towards women's health requirements and one need to question its claims of providing basic services to women under the RCH programme. Women are driven to traditional healers and/or private practitioner. Under the international conventions, which have been mentioned earlier, the state appears to be guilty of violating the reproductive rights of women. Lack of effective services during pregnancy, delivery and post-delivery, inadequate information and knowledge about contraceptives, emphasis on sterilization for spacing and ending the fertility, non-availability of diagnostic and curative services for abortion, RTI and STD etc. at PHC level amounts to deprivation of the rights to health services. Broadly, the rights that get violated are the right to liberty and security of the person, the right to privacy, the right to information and education, the right to health care and health protection, and right to the benefits of scientific progress. Low quality and poor availability of health care delivered by the government pushes poor women to utilize private, profit making and at times irrational services at a high cost leading to severe indebtedness. The state owes an obligation to make safe services available within the reach of the population. Thus, going by the meaning of human rights, women are denied the right of dignified life.

The welfare state has largely failed as we can see from the understanding that emerges from the perceptions of tribal women and service providers in the region. The central issue is that of accountability. We have seen that the legislature in the country has recognized special needs of the backward and remote tribal areas and has recommended special norm for creating health infrastructure (Bhuria Commission). The Government of Gujarat has made some successful attempts in creating this infrastructure too. However, it is the service delivery and the quality of service that has largely failed.

The problem mainly seems to lie in the top-down approach of government in planning and implementing the health programmes in general and RCH programmes in particular, which in practice seriously limits the scope of proper implementation. Despite acknowledging the community involvement in assessing its need, the government continues to implement its own agenda largely reflected in the immunization and fertility control through sterilization. It fails to create awareness among population by disseminating information and educating them to rationalize their thinking and take decision on their own. The initiative should have come from within the community towards which the state could have played the role of a facilitator. Decentralized programme does not ensure decentralized governance. How does one make way for a paradigm shift in which the state assumes the role of a facilitator rather than that of a provider? In the role of the facilitator people make their assessment by themselves and plan programmes and resource requirements. The state apparatus facilitates by providing technical and financial resources at the disposal of the communities and the service providers are at the disposal of the communities and not the governments. This approach could lead to empowerment of people.

The 'rights approach' appears to provide a better answer, as the state in case of non-response or lopsided response can be held responsible and can be hauled to the court of law for justice. The political system might also become more responsible and responsive to the needs of the communities. Women also have another disadvantage, as they are placed in a patriarchal system where they face violation of her rights in the family and society. Therefore, for a woman right to health is basic and fundamental for her healthy survival.

Notes

1. Bhagat is a traditional healer.
2. In traditional societies of India there is a belief that certain food and medicines have hot and cold properties. 'Hot' substance is believed to create heat in the body.

References

Bhattacharya, A.K. (undated). 'India's Health Care: Regulate and Perish', Business Standard, quoted in *Indian Economic Review,* Volume 2, 30th June.

Duggal, Ravi. 2005. 'Health and Health Care in Western and Central India: The Criticality of Public Finance'. *In* Parthasarathy and Iyengar (eds.) *New Development Paradigms and Challenges for Western and Central India.* New Delhi: Concept Publishing Company.

Human Rights Watch Women's Rights Project. 1998. *The Human Rights Watch; Global Report on Women's Human Rights.* New Delhi: Oxford University Press.

Hirway, Indira and Mahadevia Darshini. 2005. 'Gujarat Human Development Report 2004'. Mahatma Gandhi Labour Institute, Ahmedabad.

Government of Gujarat. 2002. Statistical Abstract of Gujarat State 2002, Directorate of Economics and Statistics, Gandhinagar.

Iyengar, Sudarshan and Ratnawali. 2004. Mapping of Reproductive Health Care Seeking Behaviour of Women and Service Provisions in Selected Tribal Areas in Gujarat. Mimeograph. Centre for Social Studies, Surat.

Kamath, Sudhir. 2004. 'Annotation on Health', *The Indian Economic Review,* Volume 2. 30th June.

Mahadevan, K. et al. 2000. 'Reproductive Health Affecting Variables of Human kind: A Conceptual Model'. *In* Mahadevan K. et al. (eds.) *Reproductive Health of Human Kind in Asia and Africa: A Global Perspective,* Vol. 1. New Delhi: B.R. Publishing Corporationp. pp. 3–49.

Ramasubban, Radhika and Shireen J. Jejeebhoy. 2000. 'Introduction.' *In* Ramasubban Radhika et al. (eds.) *Women's Reproductive Health in India*. Jaipur: Rawat Publications. pp. 13–39.

Visaria, Leela and Vimla Ramachandran. 1999. 'Overview'. *The Community Need-Based Reproductive and Child Health in India: Progress and Constraints,* Health Watch Trust, Jaipur.

Visaria, Leela et al. 2004. 'Abortion in India Emerging Issues from Qualitative Studies'. *Economic and Political Weekly*, Vol. XXXIX. Nos. 46 and 47, November 20–26, pp. 5044–52.

Index